The Button Lover's Book

Other books available from Chilton:

 Robbie Fanning, Series Editor

Contemporary Quilting Series

Fast Patch: A Treasury of Strip-Quilt Projects, by Anita Hallock

Fourteen Easy Baby Quilts, by Margaret Dittman

Machine-Quilted Jackets, Vests, and Coats, by Nancy Moore

Putting on the Glitz, by Anne Boyce and Sandra L. Hatch

The Quilter's Guide to Rotary Cutting, by Donna Poster

Speed-Cut Quilts, by Donna Poster

Creative Machine Arts Series

The Button Lover's Book, by Marilyn V. Green

Claire Shaeffer's Fabric Sewing Guide

The Complete Book of Machine Embroidery, by Robbie and Tony Fanning

Creative Nurseries Illustrated, by Debra Terry and Juli Plooster

Creative Serging Illustrated, by Pati Palmer, Gail Brown, and Sue Green

Distinctive Serger Gifts and Crafts, by Naomi Baker and Tammy Young

The Expectant Mother's Wardrobe Planner, by Rebecca Dumlao

The Fabric Lover's Scrapbook, by Margaret Dittman

Friendship Quilts by Hand and Machine, by Carolyn Vosburg Hall

Innovative Serging, by Gail Brown and Tammy Young

Innovative Sewing, by Gail Brown and Tammy Young

Owner's Guide to Sewing Machines, Sergers, and Knitting Machines, by Gale Grigg Hazen

Petite Pizzazz, by Barb Griffin

Sew, Serge, Press, by Jan Saunders

Sewing and Collecting Vintage Fashions, by Eileen MacIntosh

Simply Serge Any Fabric, by Naomi Baker and Tammy Young

Twenty Easy Machine-Made Rugs, by Jackie Dodson

Know Your Sewing Machine Series, by Jackie Dodson

Know Your Bernina, second edition

Know Your Brother, with Jane Warnick

Know Your Elna, with Carol Ahles

Know Your New Home, with Judi Cull and Vicki Lyn Hastings

Know Your Pfaff, with Audrey Griese

Know Your Sewing Machine

Know Your Singer

Know Your Viking, with Jan Saunders

Know Your Serger Series, by Naomi Baker and Tammy Young

Know Your baby lock

Know Your Pfaff Hobbylock

Know Your White Superlock

Teach Yourself to Sew Better Series, by Jan Saunders

A Step-by-Step Guide to Your Bernina

A Step-by-Step Guide to Your New Home

A Step-by-Step Guide to Your Sewing Machine

A Step-by-Step Guide to Your Viking

The Button Lover's Book

Marilyn V. Green

Creative Machine Arts Series

Chilton Book Company
Radnor, Pennsylvania

Dedication

For my family,
especially
Marguerite Tuthill Inslee
(1891–1984)
and
Suzanne Marilyn Green McPhee
(1921–1991)

Copyright © 1991 by Marilyn V. Green
All Rights Reserved

Published in Radnor, Pennsylvania
19089, by Chilton Book Company

Designed by Martha Vercoutere
Cover by Tony Jacobson
Illustrations by Marilyn V. Green
Buttons pictured in this book lent by
Kit Davies, Dagmar Dern, Marilyn V.
Green, Cate Keller, Martha Vercoutere,
and Linda Warfel

Manufactured in the United States of
America

Library of Congress Cataloging in
Publication Data
Green, Marilyn V.
    The button lover's book / Marilyn V.
Green
    p.   cm. — (Creative machine arts
series)
    Includes bibliographical references
and index.
ISBN 0-8019-8184-0 (hc)
ISBN 0-8019-8010-0 (pb)
    1. Buttons—History. 2. Buttons—
Collectors and collecting.
I. Title. II. Series.
NK3668.5.G7 1991
646'.19—dc20   90-55877
                          CIP

1 2 3 4 5 6 7 8 9 0 0 9 8 7 6 5 4 3 2 1

Contents

Odd Fact

Magician Max Malini (1873–1942) was famous for a trick that involved biting buttons from the suit coats of strangers and reaffixing the buttons before the startled victims could say "Max Malini."

Foreword

by Robbie Fanning

Amy, the four-year-old who accompanies her mom to work in our office, is a deprived child: her mother doesn't sew. Recently I gave the little sprite a bag of brightly colored buttons. She was instantly engrossed, entranced. She sorted the buttons into colors, then by holes, exclaiming when she found a no-hole button (it had a shank). She made a button road. She made a long intricate button necklace. Now she's sewing buttons on fabric scraps, learning which are too flimsy for big buttons, which are too dense for a tapestry needle.

I had intended the buttons to reside in a corporate button box, but in one day, the collection halved when Amy went home. I lacked the heart to claim ownership. We will buy more buttons.

Of the thirtysome books I've edited in the Creative Machine Arts series, this one is close to my heart. I've known Marilyn Green for 15 years. She is a personal and national treasure, bursting with information and humor about everything, including buttons.

Once you savor this book, I hope you will find your own Amy. Let there be no deprived children: give them buttons.

Acknowledgments

I am especially indebted to my editor, Robbie Fanning, for her friendship, support, frankness, and good advice.

I also am grateful to my husband, Drew McCalley, for his loving support and for never complaining about the buttons on the kitchen table and in the bathroom sink.

I also would like to thank the staffs of the Palo Alto City Library, Palo Alto, Calif. (particularly Roger Bonilla, Barbara Geibel, Ralph Libby, Sharon Olson, and Elnor Pahl); Menlo Park Public Library, Menlo Park, Calif.; and Musser Public Library, Muscatine, Iowa (particularly Barbara Bublitz) for their assistance.

Thanks also to the following helpful people: Sergei Aivazian (Consulate of the U.S.S.R., San Francisco, Calif.), Johara Alatas, Elsie Allen, Peter Banister, Julia Borne, Fred Brown (Brown's Fisheries and Shell, Muscatine, Iowa), Georgia Bryce, Debbie Casteel (Aardvark Adventures in Livermore, Calif.), Craig E.

Colten (Associate Curator of Geography at the Illinois State Museum in Springfield, Ill.), Loretta De Maio (Marketing Assistant at Simplicity Pattern Company, Inc., New York, N.Y.), Ann deWitt, Edith A. DuBose-Krieger (of the Pattern Division at Verlag Aenne Burda), Dede Evans, Patty Farber, Elayne Goodman, Deborah D. Grazier (Manager of Museum Operations at Mattatuck Museum, Waterbury, Conn.), Alexander Green, Kaitlin Green, Mitchell Green, William Green, Barb Griffin, Bernard Hahn (J and K Button Company, Muscatine, Iowa), Marian Haigh, Doris Hoover, Margot Strand Jensen, Vicki L. Johnson, Gregor Kalas (Curatorial Assistant, the Textile Museum, Washington, D.C.), Kelly Keegan (Esprit Public Relations, San Francisco, Calif.), Cate Keller, Lydia Kramer, Pamela B. Leonard (of Great American Gallery, Atlanta, Ga.), Dave and Larry Lipner (P. Lipner Button Company, Grand Rapids, Mich.), Carole Livingston (ACA JOE, San Francisco, Calif.), Barbara C. Longtin (Director, Muscatine Art Center, Muscatine, Iowa), Michele Majer (Research Assistant, the Costume Institute, Metropolitan Museum of Art, New York, N.Y.), Merrill Mason, William A. McGonagle (formerly with the Muscatine Art Center, Muscatine, Iowa), Theodore F. McKee (McKee Button Company, Muscatine, Iowa), Patricia L. McKevitt (Pendleton Woolen Mills, Portland, Ore.), Sonja Medcalf, Marilyn Merdzinski (Registrar, Grand Rapids Public Museum, Grand Rapids, Mich.), the National Archives, Dr. Karen Nelson, Steen Nottelmann (Curator, Royal Copenhagen Museum, Copenhagen), Liadain O'Donoven-Cook, Katie Obringer, Ira Ono, Fran Patterson, Gretchen Payne, Clydine Peterson, Rosalie Pfeifer, Yvonne Porcella, RickaMae, Cecilia Ridgeway, Christian Francis Roth, Shelia Schiller, Tim Scott (Chilton Book Company), Deborah S. Shinn (Assistant Curator/Decorative Arts, Cooper-Hewitt Museum, New York, N.Y.), Pat Shipley, Scott Smith (Pendleton Woolen Mills, Bellevue, Neb.), the Smithsonian Institution, J. Howard Stallings (Creative Director at After the Stork, Albuquerque, N.M.), Garlene Staton (Consumer Representative, Borden, Inc.), Dalton "Button King" Stevens, Virginia Stewart, Hugh Stix, Betty Stuntz, Martha Vercoutere, Nancy Welch, and Nicholas Westbrook (Director, Fort Ticonderoga, Ticonderoga, N.Y.).

Finally, thanks to Tony Coluzzi, Mike Lykins, and Sherman Winslow (of the Darkroom in Mountain View, Calif.) for photography tips and for the many hours they spent developing and printing my photographs.

Illustrations and photographs are by the author unless otherwise indicated.

Introduction

When I tell people that I like buttons, the first thing they're reminded of is a particular button box. The family button box is the first "toy" many of us remember. Most people begin by saying, "My grandmother (mother, aunt, or the lady down the street) let me play with her button box." Many remember a round tin box and the sound the buttons made when they shook it. Others recall a see-through button jar that glowed with a jumble of color (see Fig. Intro-1). Some remember the smell. My grandmother's button box, for example,

Intro-1

smelled (and still smells) like a mixture of plastic, sachet powder, and tailor's chalk.

But probably the best memories are of how button boxes amused so many on gloomy days. Some children sorted the buttons by color; others made button highways throughout the house or yard; and many have vivid memories of specific buttons.

If you have a grandchild, I hope you'll let him or her play with your button box. You'll be giving your grandchild a wonderful memory. Be sure to watch children under three very carefully. You don't want the child to remember the awful day he swallowed a button from his grandmother's button box.

Button boxes aren't just for children, however. Bring the family button box along the next time you visit your parents or grandparents. You'll be amazed at the memories the buttons hold. The box might contain buttons from your grandmother's wedding dress or buttons—with some fabric still attached—from your grandfather's favorite workshirt. He might tell you about the day it "disappeared." Grandmother will finally admit that she needed a nice, soft rag. Of course, she cut the buttons off first (see Fig. Intro-2).

If you don't remember a particular button box from your childhood, you can make your own. I hope this book will help get you started on your collection. For those who already have lots of buttons, I hope this book "unbuttons" some of their mysteries. As I wrote I pictured you sitting in a comfortable chair (with my book open on a table) sorting through your buttons and discovering treasures. If you find some, please write and tell me about them. I'd love to hear your button stories.

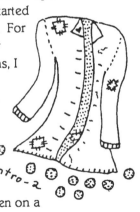

Intro-2

Marilyn V. Green

Collecting

1. Collecting Buttons

Getting Started

Whether you keep seven buttons in an ashtray on your dresser (Fig. 1-1) or an elaborate array of eighteenth-century buttons in glass display cases, you're a button collector. Buttons usually don't get thrown away; they're one in the category of things (including screws and brown paper bags) that we save because we might need one someday. Besides, buttons are very beautiful. Look down at the buttons on your shirt. Could *you* design a better button?

1-1

While most of us collect buttons just in case, many people collect them for their beauty, historical interest, monetary value, and/or for sewing projects.

Button collecting is a hobby with a long history. In the 1860s young female collectors arranged buttons in lengths known as "charm strings" or "memory strings" (Fig. 1-2). A young woman began with a "touch button" and the string grew as each friend and relative donated a special button. Glass buttons were especially popular for charm strings, which were often wrapped in tissue paper and stored in a fancy box. Legend had it that when the collector had 1,000 buttons her love would appear. (Some claim she only needed 999.) Needless to say, many women failed to reach 1,000 but still found their loves. If you find a charm string at an antique shop, don't take it apart. The strings are more valuable as is and disassembling it might jinx your love life.

1-2

Charm strings went out of fashion at the turn of the century, but button collecting is alive and well. If it interests you, the National Button Society (founded in 1938) is the club for you. To join, contact Lois Pool, Secretary, National Button Society, 2733 Juno Place, Akron, Ohio 44333-4137. The phone number is (216) 864-3296. Dues are $15 a year and include a subscription to the *National Button Bulletin*, a wonderful 100-plus page journal packed with button information. The National Button Society has local chapters in most states; contact the national headquarters for the current address of the chapter nearest your home.

If you're interested in getting more involved in button collecting, go to the public library and check out books about buttons. *The Collector's Encyclopedia of Buttons*, by Sally C. Luscomb (see the Bibliography), is good for beginners. If you live in the Midwest, the National Button Society has a useful library in Akron, Ohio. Sadly, many of the best books on button collecting are out of print.

Button conventions are also great places to learn about buttons. Button collectors are friendly and eager to talk about their hobby. The National Button Society hosts an annual convention, as does each state chapter. The *National Button Bulletin* contains a calendar of events that includes these meetings.

At the conventions, button collections are displayed in wooden frames called "trays." They are arranged by type of material or subject matter to make it easy to decide what to collect. Judges award prizes for the best trays, which often are photographed for the *National Button Bulletin*. The photos appear in the magazine with captions such as "Award-Winning Tray at Moline."

National Button Society members often specialize in a particular type of button, such as shoe-shaped buttons or buttons from military uniforms. The rules for displaying buttons are strict and precise. For example, the rule for the pastimes, games, and sports category is: "Buttons appropriate in this class should include people and action in their designs. Sporting equipment such as golf clubs or tennis racquets are appropriate as pictorial objects; hunting dogs and game subjects, as animal life."

1-3

Pity the poor person who entered a tray in the animal heads category at the 1989 meeting of the California Button Society. His arrangement included a fish-shaped button and assorted animal heads. He didn't win, but he did receive a terse explanation from the judge: "Fish has body, should be head only" (Fig. 1-3).

Other button categories include french tights (a type of nineteenth-century brass button); cherubs; gnomes and fairies; people (assorted); fruits (assorted); transportation (nonhuman); and moonglows (a type of glass button). Interestingly enough, carved netsuke (a toggle used to fasten a small pouch or purse to a kimono sash) also rates a category.

Where to Find Buttons

If you ask button collectors where they find buttons, they are likely to tell you anywhere and everywhere.

Start with your own, your mother's, or your grandmother's button box. Collectors obtain some of their most prized buttons from family members or friends. Let people know you love buttons and they'll sometimes invite you to go through their button boxes.

Purchase old buttons at antique shows and shops, as well as at some fabric and coin shops. If you don't see buttons, always ask. Shop owners often have some tucked in a drawer. Some mail-order button dealers carry antique buttons; consult the list of Mail-Order Sources for Buttons in the Appendices. My favorite mail-order sources for old buttons are Ornamental Resources and Renaissance Buttons. Button dealers also advertise in the *National Button Bulletin*.

Never pass up the chance to buy someone's button box at a garage sale, rummage sale, or thrift shop. This is where I've found many of my favorite treasures, and I always feel lucky to be the new owner. These button boxes usually are not just home to buttons. The last one I bought also contained bits

of broken jewelry; a few real pearls; a 1917 penny; a thimble; marbles; and miscellaneous hooks, eyes, and snaps (Fig. 1-4).

I've even found some good buttons in the street! (I know. We don't know *where* those buttons have been.) By the end of a tour of Russia several years ago, however, I had everyone on the trip looking down to find "buttons for Marilyn." Some of those "found" buttons are very special (Fig. 1-5).

Buy new buttons at fabric shops. Some art galleries and craft shops stock handmade buttons. A number of buttonmakers and button dealers sell their wares by mail. Consult the list of Mail-Order Sources for Buttons in the Appendices and send for samples and catalogs.

In addition to competitions and lectures about buttons, button conventions also feature button dealers. The dealers usually occupy a huge room in which the sound—a sort of rolling, scratching sound similar to that at the seashore—is amazing. This sound is made by people pawing through what button collectors call "poke boxes" (large boxes full of buttons for sale) (Fig. 1-6).

Fig. 1-6 Dealers' "poke boxes" at button conventions often contain treasures.

Button prices range from twenty-five cents to more than $100. Veteran collectors are particular about their purchases. A tiny nick or dent can lessen the value of a button, so collectors often carry loupes or magnifying glasses with which to examine buttons. Knowledgeable people look at the back of each button for clues about its age and method of construction.

Fig. 1-7 *My baseball player had a red hat and socks painted on when I bought him.*

Buttons that have been "altered" also are worth less to some collectors. For example, button collector Dorothy Stimson, writing in the *National Button Bulletin*, tells the story of a collector who searched for years for a particular set of buttons shaped like baseball players (Fig. 1-7). She finally corresponded with another collector who was willing to sell her set. When the buttons arrived, she was miffed; her precious baseball player buttons had been ruined. It seems the woman she'd purchased the buttons from had painted pants on the players. "Didn't want those men in my house without their pants on," she explained.

Follow the advice of veteran button collector Sonja Medcalf: "Start your collection with small modern buttons that you like. Learn about how they were constructed and about the materials used to make them before you get into expensive buttons. Don't buy a button just because the guy next to you says, "This is great." Buy what you like. In other words, if you like baseball players with pants, go ahead and paint.

Odd Fact

In 1892, preacher Joe Toler of rural Ben Creek, West Virginia, arrived home to find most of the buttons neatly severed from the clothing hanging in his home. Also missing was a roll of twenty-five

silver dollars. His explanation for the thefts? "It had to be someone doped up, or a member of a cult, or someone who is demon-possessed." Or maybe a button lover?

2. Sorting and Storing Buttons

❀ ❀ ❀

Sorting Buttons

Each button collector has his or her own system for sorting and storing buttons. Many sort them according to

material (fabric, metal, glass, enamel, pearl, and so on), using a cardboard egg carton or another box with compartments, and then store each category together. Some collectors sort buttons according to subject matter.

Under this system, for example, all buttons embellished with or shaped like cats are stored together (Fig. 2-1).

Make up an organizational system that will work for you. Think about how you will be using the buttons and keep that in mind when setting up a system for storing them. You want to be able to put your finger on that tassel-shaped button when you need it.

Those of us who use buttons for sewing often separate them by color. My own categories are red, blue, yellow, orange, purple, pink, black, brown, white (plastic), white (mother-of-pearl), metal, leather, wood, clear, fabric, and "special" buttons (Fig. 2-2).

Fig. 2-2 *I store buttons by color in lidless plastic boxes. Identical buttons are strung on plastic-coated telephone wire.*

Storing the Buttons You Use

What kind of box is best for the buttons? The main consideration is humidity; store buttons in a dry space with a fairly constant temperature. Buttons must breathe, so it's best to store them in a ventilated box. Memories aside, metal tins are not recommended because they can rust and damage the metal buttons stored within.

Don't store buttons in a garage or basement, and *never* store plastic buttons and metal buttons in the same box. Plastic sometimes deteriorates and gets sticky; that moisture can cause some metal buttons to rust.

I store all but my metal buttons in lidless, see-through plastic boxes. I use a wooden box for metal buttons. Plastic cabinets with numerous drawers (sold for storing screws and other hardware) also are ideal (Fig. 2-3). P. Lipner

and Company, a button business in Grand Rapids, Michigan, uses cardboard archival storage boxes with buttons mounted on the lids to indicate what's inside (Fig. 2-4).

Fig. 2-3 *Many types of containers are suitable for button storage. Pictured here are a many-drawer hardware cabinet, plastic storage box, glass candy jar, wooden boxes, and an old jewelry box. Metal containers are not suitable.*

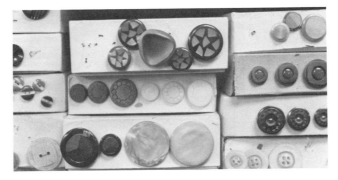

Fig. 2-4 *Some button shops store buttons in archival storage boxes with buttons mounted on the front to show what's inside.*

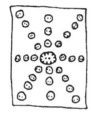
Handmade fabric-covered boxes are ideal for storing buttons. Many fabric-covered boxes are padded and provide cushioning for fragile buttons. Consider constructing your own box. There are several excellent box-making books, but my favorite is *Embroidered Boxes and Other Construction Techniques* by Jane Lemon (Batsford/David and Charles, 1987). To purchase this book, write to Sterling Publishing Company, 387 Park Ave. S., New York, NY 10016-8810. Check your local library for other titles.

For a list of dealers who sell button boxes by mail, consult Other Button Resources in the Appendices.

Storing Collectible Buttons

Collectors who enter competitions store and display their buttons on 9" x 12" cards made from pebble or railroad board, available at art supply stores (Fig. 2-5). White is most common, but other colors also are acceptable.

If you plan to enter a competition, contact the National Button Society (NBS) before mounting your buttons. Ask for a copy of the *Official NBS Classification for Competition Rules*. These rules specify the sizes and types of buttons that can be displayed together. The National Button Society also sells button measures to assist in determining the size of a button.

If you don't want to make your own mounts, attractive button mounting cards are available by mail from Barbara J. Rodgers. (Her address is 440 W. Beaver St., Hellam, PA 17406. The phone number is (717) 757-5720. Send a business-sized self-addressed, stamped envelope for information.) Ms. Rodgers offers five designs: Country

2-5

Floral, Noah's Ark, Peddler Bunny, Floral Hearts, and
Romanesque. Other cards are available from Phil
Linley. (His address is 232 Linley Dr., Fairfield, CT
06430.)

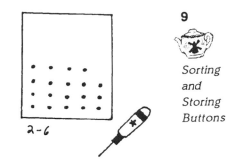

To mount the buttons, use an awl to punch holes
(one or two for each button) in an attractive arrangement on the railroad or pebble board (Fig. 2-6). Then
attach the buttons through the holes with plastic-
coated telephone wire (Fig. 2-7) obtained from a

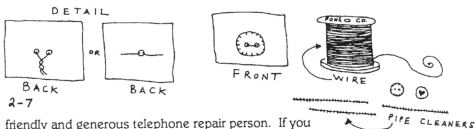

friendly and generous telephone repair person. If you
can't obtain telephone wire, any flexible wire that can
be threaded through the buttonholes will do. Spools of
wire are sold in hardware stores. Some people use
pipe cleaners, but they rust in humid climates.

Many collectors keep their button cards in plastic or
paper sleeves and store them in file cabinets. Others
keep them in loose-leaf notebooks or albums.

Unmounted buttons can be pinned to velvet, which,
when rolled and tied with a ribbon, cushions and
protects the buttons (Fig. 2-8).

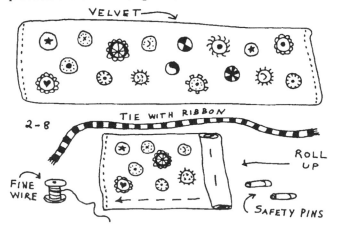

Mount special buttons in frames and display them on the wall. Many collectors call these frames "trays." Wooden button display frames are available from Mack and Mary's. (The address is 63 Bacon St., Meriden, CT 06450. The phone number is (203) 235-7858. Send a business-sized self-addressed, stamped envelope for information.) Buttons can

be displayed on their own or combined with lace, fabric, or special objects from the same period to create a collage (Figs. 2-9 and 2-10). Artist Marian Haigh includes buttons in her collages and ceramic pieces (plates 3B and 15B).

Prairie Pedlar, a mail-order business in Lyons, Kansas, often centers an old button on fabric from

Fig. 2-9 Artist (Tampa, Florida) buttons, photographs, of-a-kind collage pins. This Photograph courtesy of the

Linda Newman uses antique and frames in her one-piece measures 2" x 1 1/2". artist.

Fig. 2-10 Idle Dreams of Things That Cannot Be *(36" x 48") by Elayne Goodman of Columbus, Mississippi, features wooden cigar boxes, frames, small antiques, old photographs, lace, beads, and lots of buttons. Photograph by Frank Roberts and courtesy of the artist.*

the same period and displays it along-
side the button's story (Fig. 2-11).

Quilters Jane Burch Cochran
(plates 3A and 15A; Fig. 2-12), Merrill

Fig. 2-11 The Prairie Pedlar mounts
antique buttons on informative cards that
provide information on button history.
Each card comes with a mailing envelope.

Fig. 2-12 Detail of For All Our Grandmothers *quilt by Jane Burch Cochran (see Plate 3A).*
Cochran began using buttons several years ago when she bought a gallon jar filled with
buttons for $5 at a flea market. Photograph courtesy of the Great American Gallery,
Atlanta, Georgia.

Mason (plate 16A), Fran Patterson (plate 8B), and Yvonne Porcella (Fig. 2-13) all use buttons on their art quilts. Following their lead, I mounted my special buttons (the ones that are "too good to use") on an old quilt top that hangs in our dining room (Fig. 2-14). I

Fig. 2-13 Americana Enshrined *(36" x 38") by Yvonne Porcella of Modesto, California, 1989. Photograph by Sharon Risedorph. Porcella was the curator of the 1989 quilt exhibit "Americana Enshrined." Her quilt celebrates "the essense of typically American 'stuff.'" Photograph courtesy of the Great American Gallery, Atlanta, Georgia.*

Fig. 2-14 *We never tire of looking at my button quilt. I continue to add special buttons given to me by friends and bits of embroidery from my travels. When this quilt is full, I'll start another!*

also included bits of embroidery from my travels. It's a wonderful way to display the treasures that often get stuffed in a drawer (Fig. 2-15). Buttons also are effective on decorative pillows (Fig. 2-16).

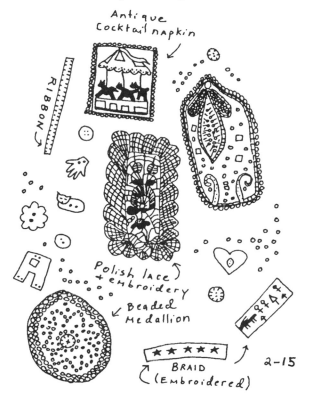

Fig. 2-16 The cat pillow was a gift; I embellished it with buttons. The fabric fish was originally a purse. I stuffed it and added button "scales."

You also can attach buttons to a wreath frame (available at craft supply shops) with fine wire. It takes a lot of buttons to make a wreath, but the effect

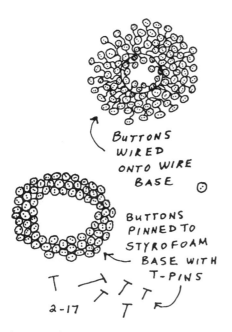

BUTTONS
WIRED
ONTO WIRE
BASE

BUTTONS
PINNED TO
STYROFOAM
BASE WITH
T-PINS

2-17

is marvelous (Fig. 2-17). If you don't have enough buttons to cover a naked frame, use wire to scatter some among the greenery on a plain evergreen wreath (Fig. 2-18).

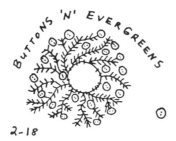

BUTTONS 'N' EVERGREENS

2-18

Some furniture stores carry glass display cabinets or tables shaped like glass boxes that can be used to display buttons (Fig. 2-19). Artist Elayne Goodman covered an entire dresser with buttons (Fig. 2-20).

If you really want to go wild with your buttons, follow the lead of Bishopville, South Carolina's, Dalton "Button King" Stevens. Not only has he covered his guitar and car with buttons, but he also plans to take buttons with him when he dies. His coffin is covered with them. I forgot to ask if he'll be "buttoned in" (Fig. 2-21).

Finally, if you have buttons you no longer need, sew them to a large piece of felt and use it as a substitute for wrapping paper (Fig. 2-22). Create a glittering, sumptuous wrap with metal buttons or a playful wrap for a child's gift with large, primary-colored or animal-shaped buttons.

♥ WRAPPING "PAPERS" ♥

MULTI-COLORED BUTTONS

CAT BUTTONS

METAL BUTTONS
2-22   ON GREY FELT

Fig. 2-19 *(left) A glass-topped display table enables you to enjoy your special buttons every day. I often change my display for holidays, featuring red and green buttons at Christmas and orange and black buttons at Halloween.*

Fig. 2-20 *(right)* Vanity for the Very Vain *(82" x 40" x 18")* by Elayne Goodman of Columbus, Mississippi. "An elderly vanity is painted white. It is crusted with designs in buttons glued in place." Photograph by Frank Roberts and courtesy of the artist.

Fig. 2-21 *Dalton "Button King" Stevens has put Bishopville, South Carolina, on the map by covering his musical instruments, car, coffin, and toilet (not pictured) with buttons! Photograph by Express Printing and Photography, Lugoff, South Carolina, courtesy of his highness.*

History

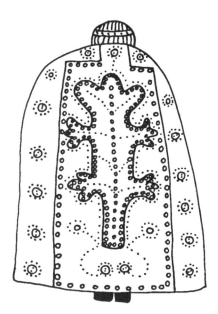

3. Button History

Many people are curious about which buttons are the most valuable. I usually answer, "Those that you like best." In terms of monetary value, however, old buttons usually are more valuable than new ones. As with most antiques, rare pieces are the most valuable. For example, many collectors would pay a great deal for a button made to commemorate the inaugurations of George Washington because not many of these buttons exist. Buttons set with real jewels, such as diamonds and pearls, also are very dear. Old buttons made from fragile materials may be valuable simply because they've survived.

One of the joys of button collecting is learning about their rich history. The history of buttons parallels the history of fashion, the availability and popularity of various buttonmaking materials, and the history of manufacturing.

The following is a brief history of buttons classified alphabetically by material. For information on identifying and caring for these buttons, consult Identifying Button Materials and Button Care in the Appendices.

Antler and Horn

Many early American buttons were made from antler and horn (the hooves and other horny parts of cattle and related animals). In the early days of this country, horn buttons sometimes were made out of scraps left over from the manufacture of combs and other household objects. Antler buttons often were manufactured by indi-viduals working at home with simple tools.

Horn buttons still are made from the hooves of buffalo and cattle. The modern buttons don't have the same rich color and complex markings as those made many years ago, however. Some say it's because today's animals graze on inferior grass.

Bone

Bone is one of the earliest known materials used for making buttons. A Stone Age bone button was found by archaeologists digging in the Grotte des Morts in Garde,

STONE AGE
BONE BUTTON
FRANCE
3-1

France (Fig. 3-1). Small bone objects that may have been buttons also were found in Egyptian tombs dating from the

Sixth Dynasty. Button-shaped objects made of bone also were worn as pendants by the men of Phoenicia (3000 B.C.). Experts do not believe that any of these early buttons were used as fasteners.

Some claim that bone buttons first were used for fastening garments in twelfth-century France. In the fourteenth century bone buttons were made by French beadmakers.

In the nineteenth century, sheep and cattle bone buttons were made all over the British Isles. Many early bone buttons were cut on a lathe and fitted with metal shanks; others were drilled with two, three, or four holes. The sew-through buttons often were used on underwear. Bone sometimes was also carved elaborately to simulate ivory.

Ceramic

Odd Fact

Legendary Life *magazine photographer Alfred Eisenstaedt was once a belt and button salesman.*

Many of the famous European porcelain manufactories have made and/or still make buttons. According to Steen Nottelmann, curator of the Royal Copenhagen Museum in Copenhagen, Royal Copenhagen first produced porcelain buttons (in several sizes and models) in 1783. Around the same time, English ceramicist Josiah Wedgwood manufactured cameolike buttons that were mounted in metal bezels. Other well-known factories that produced buttons include Minton, Delft, Limoges, Meissen, and Sèvres. Few of these buttons have survived, and they are valuable to collectors.

During the German occupation of Paris in World War II, popular buttonmaking materials, such as metal and leather, were in short supply. Hence, huge ceramic buttons became fashionable. Some of the most whimsical ceramic buttons were made between 1938 and 1940 by artist Marguerite Stix (plate 2B). Stix, who studied ceramics at Vienna's Wiener Werkstatte, designed buttons for Parisian couturiere Elsa Schiaparelli.

Some of today's most imaginative handmade buttons are ceramic. Many button craftspeople sell their wares at craft fairs and by mail. Consult Mail-Order Sources for Buttons in the Appendices. Most buttonmakers will send samples for a nominal charge.

I'm especially fond of the porcelain buttons designed by Arel Heilman Mishory of The Hands Work in Pecos, New Mexico, located thirty miles east of Santa Fe. In fact, if you're interested in seeing porcelain buttonmaking, Arel and her business partner/husband, Mark, welcome visitors to their studio during business hours. Please call at least one day in advance to arrange your visit. The Hands Work's full address and phone number are included in the Mail-Order Sources for Buttons listing in the Appendices.

Covered

Seventeenth- and eighteenth-century buttonmakers didn't have convenient button-covering kits to assist them in making fabric-covered buttons for the fashionable, elaborately embroidered clothing of the day. Buttonmaking was an art, and to learn it aspiring buttonmakers apprenticed themselves to master lacemakers and embroiderers.

In France, a student of *passementerie* (fancy trimmings made of braid, cord, gimp, beading, and metallic threads in various combinations) served an apprenticeship of nine years before opening his own business. Buttonmakers belonged to the same guild as lacemakers. Louis XV had a servant whose only job was making buttons.

These early covered buttons were made over wooden, bone, or mother-of-pearl molds and sometimes were embellished with pearls, beads, sequins, and jewels (Fig. 3-2).

Another notable variety of covered buttons was made (from the end of the seventeenth century to the

Odd Fact

Button Gwinnett (1735–1777) signed the Declaration of Independence, but not much else. His signature is very valuable to autograph collectors because he was mortally wounded in a duel less than a year after signing the famous document. Other papers bearing his signature are extremely rare.

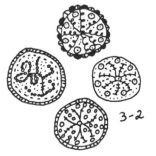

3-2

middle of the nineteenth century) in Dorsetshire, England (Fig. 3-3). A

SOME DORSET
thread buttons
look like
tiny donuts.   3-3

particularly attractive type of Dorset thread button was made by lacemakers who covered wire rings with delicate, weblike patterns of hair, silk, and/or wool. Most Dorset thread buttons were made in private homes. The buttons were used primarily for women's dresses and underwear.

In the 1920s satin buttons, painted to resemble cartoon star Betty Boop, were worn on ladies' garters. Those pictured here are made of plastic (Fig. 3-4).

Fig. 3-4 Flapper buttons were popular on women's underwear in the 1920s. These are attached to pencils. Author's collection. Gift from Dede Evans.

Bridal gowns traditionally have included rows of tiny covered buttons. For example, White House bride Lynda Johnson Robb's wedding dress had forty-six buttons.

Crocheted

Crocheted buttons were popular in France and Ireland at the turn of the century. The "French knob," a hard, ball-shaped crocheted button, was often worn by French prostitutes. Button historian Primrose Peacock believes that this prevented other Parisians from using crocheted buttons.

Glass

The first fine glass buttons were made in the eighteenth century. Since then, buttons have been made with nearly every glassmaking process. Britain's Queen Victoria, who wore mourning clothes from 1861 (the year Prince Albert died) until her death in 1901, popularized black glass buttons. Most of these buttons were made in Venice.

Button collectors specialize in two types of glass buttons: black glass and clear or colored glass. Paperweight buttons are especially popular and were manufactured by many of the world's most highly regarded glassmaking facilities, such as Clichy in France.

Ivory

Carved ivory buttons were first made in Japan, Italy, and China in the nineteenth century.

True ivory is obtained primarily in Africa from the tusks of elephants. It now is illegal to import ivory from the African elephant to the United States.

The teeth and tusks of several other animals—including the whale, hippopotamus, and walrus—also are sold as ivory. A natural and beautiful substitute is vegetable ivory (tagua).

Jet

Jet is a black variety of the mineral lignite (brown coal). A great quantity of the substance was mined from bituminous shales in Yorkshire, England. It is no longer mined and was seldom used for buttons. Most buttons that look like jet are actually black glass.

Knotted/Frogs

A frog is an amphibian, but it's also an ornamental fastener consisting of a knotted or conventional button and an often-elaborate loop through which the button passes. Frogs probably originated in China and were introduced in the West, where they first were used primarily on military uniforms in the eighteenth century.

How this fastening got its name is unclear. The name "frog" is possibly derived from the Portuguese *froco* (a tuft of wool or silk). Other scholars believe the term is derived from the Latin *floccus* (a flock of wool).

Originally, a frog was a belt loop used for transporting a weapon, but the word eventually acquired a broader meaning. For example, a writer for the *New England Weekly Journal* referred to ornamental fastenings in 1736 as "new Fashion'd Frogs." Frogs are also sometimes known as Brandenburgs (circa 1770).

Leather

Leather buttons have been made since the Middle Ages, when, according to some, they were made by bookbinders. In early America leather buttons were made in the workshops of harnessmakers and shoemakers.

Metal

Throughout history, metal has been the most common button material.

The earliest metal "buttons" may have been used on belts and other leather objects in the Bavarian Alps during the Bronze Age (circa 3500 B.C.). Not buttons in the current sense of the word, these ancient metal fastenings are similar to metal studs often used on modern leather garments (Fig. 3-5). Late in the nineteenth century, German archaeologist Heinrich Schliemann (1822–1890) found golden buttons from about 1500 B.C. at Mycenae in Greece, but there is no conclusive evidence to suggest that they were used as buttons are today.

Metal buttons used as fasteners probably first appeared in the thirteenth or fourteenth centuries. They were first manufactured from less-precious metals, but jewelers soon began turning out buttons of silver and gold. Scottish warriors reportedly wore heavy silver buttons on their kilts, which were used to pay for their funerals.

During the Renaissance golden buttons set with jewels often were made by goldsmiths working in monasteries. For years these fancy buttons were the rage of European royalty. France's Francis I (1494–1547), who could be described as a button maniac, even invited the great Italian goldsmith Cellini to Paris to make buttons (among other things). According to French courtier Saint-Simon, Louis XIV (1638–1715) wore so many heavily jeweled buttons that he nearly "sank beneath the weight of them."

Mass-produced die-stamped metal buttons, such as those used on uniforms, were first made in the early part of the nineteenth century in England (mostly in Birmingham).

In the early days of America, buttons made from coins (often Spanish dollars) were worn on men's clothing and traded with Native Americans. Brass buttons were manufactured by Casper Wister of Philadelphia as early as 1750. Silversmith Paul Revere (1735–1818) is believed to have made silver buttons in his workshop.

Beginning in 1802 in Waterbury, Connecticut, the firm of Abel Porter and Company began mass-producing copper buttons. The metal was obtained from "worn out stills and sugar boilers, old kettles, copper

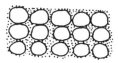

BRONZE AGE BUTTONS FROM LEATHER OBJECTS 3-5

Plate 1 *Many button companies employed artists to produce posters and button cards. This chromolithograph advertised the pearl buttons manufactured by the Boepple Button Company of Muscatine, Iowa, circa 1900. Photograph courtesy of the Muscatine Art Center, Muscatine, Iowa.*

Plate 2A *Sew a row of buttons on each side of a garment; a cord laced between these buttons holds the dress closed.*

Plate 2B *In 1938-1939, Marguerite Stix made ceramic buttons for fashion designer Elsa Schiaparelli. The buttons are now in the collection of the Costume Institute at the Metropolitan Museum of Art in New York City. Photograph courtesy of Hugh Stix.*

Plate 3A For All Our Grandmothers *(45" wide by 60" high) by Jane Burch Cochran of Rabbit Hash, Kentucky, 1989. The artist sewed special mementos (obtained from her grandmothers, her mother's favorite grandmother, and friends' grandmothers) to this quilt. The paint brush, for example, is from her artist grandmother. Cochran also included a pin that her other grandmother received for hospital volunteer work. Photograph courtesy of the artist.*

Plate 3B Button Basket *(24" diam. by 4" deep) by Marian Haigh of Austin, Texas, 1987. Haigh has made several button baskets. This one is constructed of sawdust-fired clay embellished with old buttons and wire. Of making the button baskets she says, "The whole time I was saying to myself, 'Yuck, what am I doing sewing plastic buttons on clay!' But I am so glad I did. I was really moving forward with lots of experimental work." Photograph by Phyllis Frede and courtesy of the artist.*

Plate 4 An assortment of practical and collectible buttons made from different materials (identified from the top, left to right).
Row 1: bone, antler, ceramic (3), Baker's clay, acrylic modeling compound.
Row 2: fabric covered, crocheted, glass, horn (2), ivory.
Row 3: jet, knotted, leather, bottle cap, brass.
Row 4: pewter, silver, steel, plastic (4).
Row 5: rhinestone, rubber (2), shell, tortoiseshell, wood.

Fig. 3-6 *Silver buttons made by Native Americans embellish Frank Cushing's outfit. Born in Pennsylvania, Frank Hamilton Cushing (1857–1900) was adopted by a Zuni tribe, made a member of the Macaw Clan and given the sacred name "Medicine Flower." Photograph (circa 1880–1884) courtesy of the Smithsonian Institution (photo number: Portraits 22-E).*

sheathing and the like."[1] The firm advertised "triple, double and single gilt coat and vest buttons, in every variety of shapes, forms, and colors, and military and naval buttons, according to sample."[2]

Collectors consider the metal buttons made for delegates to George Washington's first and second inaugurations to be the ultimate find. Twenty-two different patterns exist. If you have an authentic Washington inaugural button, you could sell it and buy yourself a nice car. Be wary, however. Many counterfeit copies have been made and it's very unusual to find an original.

It also should be noted that the earliest silver buttons made by Native Americans in the American Southwest were made from silver coins (Fig. 3-6). These buttons often were used as currency and pawned in exchange for necessities. Pawned silver was held by the trader until redeemed by the maker; silver not redeemed within a specified time was sold. Silver buttons marked "pawn" are not necessarily better than those that are not, however. The craftspeople often kept the best pieces for personal use.

French designer Coco Chanel (1883-1971) used metal buttons on many of her garments. Many were embossed with personal icons: her profile, initials, signs of the zodiac (Leo, the Lion), or good luck symbols (a four-leaf clover). In fact, the House of Chanel (under Karl Lagerfeld) still is using special metal buttons. The fall 1990 collection featured a garment with jeweled, egg-shaped buttons costing $180 each—and that's just for the buttons.

Plastic

The first plastic, Parkesine, was invented in 1862 in England, but it never replaced natural materials in the manufacture of buttons. More important to the button industry was New Jersey resident John Wesley Hyatt's invention of another plastic ten years later. Hyatt's celluloid was first used for billiard balls, but it soon became popular as an inexpensive substitute for ivory, bone, tortoiseshell, amber, and horn in the manufacture of buttons and other household articles.

An enormous number of plastics have been used for buttons, and it's extremely difficult to identify specific plastics. One of the most popular plastics with button collectors is Bakelite. This hard thermoset plastic, invented between 1907 and 1909 by Belgian-American chemist Leo Hendrik Baekeland, often was used for buttons. Bakelite (the generic name is phenolic) is considered the forerunner of modern plastics. Bakelite often was used to simulate amber. Phenolic plastics became extremely popular for buttons in the 1930s. These buttons are

relatively easy to find because phenolic is tough and many buttons have survived.

When plastic buttons are molded in the shape of realistic items, such as shoes or French poodles (Fig. 3-7), they're known as realistics, moderns, or goofies.

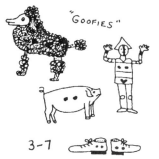

3-7

Today, many plastic buttons are made from polyester resin. The liquid resin is whirled in steel drums until it solidifies into flexible sheets that can be lifted. Round button slugs are then stamped out of the sheets (Fig. 3-8) and machine finished. Holes are drilled and the buttons are polished in tumblers (often filled with ground corncobs).

The buttons often are custom-dyed to match a

specific fabric provided to the button factory by a clothing manufacturer. Dyes usually are added to the liquid resin, but sometimes the finished buttons are colored. The buttons are popular with clothing manufacturers because plastic is cheaper and more durable than most natural materials, such as mother-of-pearl.

Plastic buttons are made all over the world. For example, Qiaotou produces most of China's buttons. This town of 25,000 has 900 button factories.

Fig. 3-8 *A modern Muscatine, Iowa, button factory uses Italian-made machinery to punch slugs for plastic buttons.*

Shell

Your button box probably contains a lot of buttons made from mother-of-pearl. Many people think of these as ordinary, white shirt buttons. I've always considered them special, probably because they seem old-fashioned and handmade.

At first glance, white mother-of-pearl buttons all might look much the same. There are actually two types: those made from freshwater clams and those made from ocean shells. To my eye, freshwater pearl buttons often are glossier and more opaque than ocean pearl buttons. For example, imagine the look of hand-pulled taffy and compare that to a piece of glossy butterscotch and you'll have the idea.

 # Freshwater Pearl

Freshwater pearl buttons are no longer made. But from 1892 until the 1960s, freshwater pearl buttons were manufactured along the Mississippi River and its tributaries.

At its height, the industry was profitable, thriving, and colorful. John Frederick Boepple, a German immigrant, is credited with recognizing the button potential in Mississippi River shells. According to local folklore, Boepple cut his foot on a piece of shell in Iowa's Sangamon River. Since he'd worked as a turner in Germany and created buttons and other ornamental treasures from shells, animal horn, tortoiseshell, and vegetable ivory, he decided to see what he could do with freshwater shells.

At the time American buttonmakers made buttons from metal, bone, cloth, and ocean shells. The shell buttons were the most popular and also the most expensive. Boepple experimented and found that he could make beautiful, less expensive buttons from freshwater clam shells.

Hoping for financial backing, he showed the buttons to business-people in Muscatine, Iowa. William Molis, superintendent of the Muscatine Water Works, expressed an interest in the project, and he and Boepple opened the world's first freshwater pearl button factory.

Others followed suit, and the Mississippi River town became the "Freshwater Pearl Button Capital of the World." By 1910, Muscatine had forty-three button factories, and nearly half of the town's 3,500 wage earners were buttonmakers.

Fig. 3-9 Unidentified man
in a flat-bottomed
clamming boat on the
Mississippi River near
Muscatine, Iowa (circa
1905). The dangling,
four-pronged metal
hooks—called
"crowfeet"—were dragged
on the river bottom to snag
freshwater clams. The
many varieties had
colorful common names
such as Monkey-Face,
Pocketbook, and Higgin's
Eye. Photograph from the
Oscar Grossheim Glass
Plate Negative Collection,
Musser Public Library,
Muscatine, Iowa.
Photograph courtesy of
the Musser Public Library.

Throughout the Midwest rivers were crowded with
small, flat-bottomed clam boats (Fig. 3-9). In the
summertime clamming families camped in tents and
wooden shanties along the river shores. Children and
adults worked together steaming the clams, removing
the meats, and sorting the many varieties of shells.

Round blanks then were drilled from the shells (Fig.
3-10) and sold to the button factories, where they were

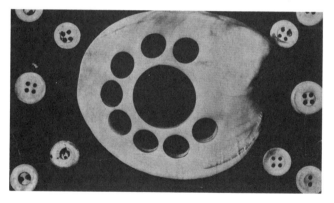

Fig. 3-10 The holes in the freshwater clam shell indicate
that slugs were cut from the shell to make buttons.
William A. McGonagle, formerly with the Muscatine Art
Center, told me that the former owner of his home in
Muscatine was a button cutter, so the yard is littered with
shells like this one. "They rise up out of the ground after
it rains; it's spooky because the shells look like little
skulls. The slug holes are the 'eyes'," said Mr.
McGonagle. Postcard photograph from the author's
collection.

polished and drilled. Nearly everything was done by hand. Work in a button factory was not pleasant. The noise from the polishing and drilling machines was deafening and the smell was overwhelming (Fig. 3-11).

Some of the button finishing was done in Muscatine's private homes. Women often were supplied with buttons and cardboard button cards. The buttons then were sewn onto the cards by hand. In 1911 pay for carding buttons was about $10 a week (plate 1).

Gradually, the industry no longer could compete with cheaper and more durable plastic buttons. Factories began to close, and the ones that remained no longer could afford to make freshwater pearl buttons. In 1957, when the McKee Button Company discontinued manufacture of pearl buttons, the remaining slugs and buttons were thrown into the company parking lot, where they remain (Fig. 3-12).

Today McKee Button Company is one of Muscatine's few surviving button factories. It and two other factories now manufacture plastic buttons, primarily for large shirt manufacturers. Gone are the

Fig. 3-12 When the McKee Button Company stopped making freshwater pearl buttons, the remaining stock was dumped in the company parking lot.

Fig. 3-11 Female workers sorting and sewing buttons on cards in a Muscatine, Iowa, button factory circa 1917. Photograph courtesy of the National Archives, Washington, D.C. (photo number: 22 MPB-907).

福

days when Ronald Reagan chose Muscatine's annual "Pearl Button Queen" from photographs sent to him of seven local button factory employees (1946). The last freshwater pearl button factory closed in Muscatine in 1969.

It should be noted that actual pearls seldom were used to make buttons. In the 1960s, however, a curious connection developed between the clamming industry along the Mississippi River and the Japanese cultured pearl industry. The freshwater clam shells, once used for pearl buttons, now are sold to Japanese oyster farmers. They implant tiny freshwater clamshell pellets in ocean oysters, which helps produce fine cultured pearls.

Ocean Pearl

Shell buttons of exceptional beauty and quality were manufactured in the eighteenth and nineteenth centuries. In the mid-nineteenth century, Paris was the center for buttons made from ocean shell. French buttonmakers were especially adept at transforming shells into engraved and pierced buttons. Buttons also were embellished with cut steel or jewels. Each button was unique.

At this time mother-of-pearl buttons also were manufactured in Germany and England. In Birmingham, England, more than 2,000 people were employed in the button industry. The shells used in button manufacturing were not found locally; they came from the Philippines, the Bay of Panama, the Red Sea, and the Persian Gulf. The most prized shell, the white macassar, came from the East Indies. The raw materials sometimes were shipped in mahogany crates, often as ballast on ships returning from the Orient. So many shell buttons were manufactured in Birmingham that the town hall reportedly rests on tons of mollusk shells.

George Washington (1732–1799) reportedly owned several sets of shell buttons. Ocean pearl buttons, however, were not introduced in quantity to the United States until around 1855. At that time buttons made from shells gathered in Australia were especially desirable.

By 1908 the ocean pearl button industry was thriving in Japan. Shells were shipped from the Ryukyu Islands, Formosa, South Sea Islands, Dutch East Indies, Ise, and Omura to Kobe and Osaka on sailing ships. Early newspaper accounts mention five large button factories in Kobe and Osaka and some eighty smaller shops in Osaka and the Kavansai district.

Small shops also were located in Kyoto, Okayama, and Kyushu. One factory in Kobe employed over 150 workers. Each worker specialized in a single procedure and was paid according to the number and quality of the buttons he or she produced. Button shaping and cutting was done almost exclusively by women. All workers owned their own tools. Buttons were carded in private homes, mostly by women who sewed the buttons (two stitches per button) to foil and/or blue paper.

Just prior to World War II, a great deal of ocean pearl was harvested from Australian waters by Japanese divers. Nearly all the pearling equipment was sunk by the Allies during the war, and recovery of the industry was slow and difficult. The price of raw materials soared to nearly double what it was before the war.

Postwar harvests were conducted in deep tropical waters off northern Australia and near the Philippines and India. The Japanese were barred from diving for ocean shells, but Japanese fishermen, who were considered especially brave and skillful, often trained other divers.

Because pearl buttonmaking is highly labor intensive, most of today's ocean pearl buttons are made in Japan and the Philippines, where labor costs are low. Buttons still are made in much the same manner.

Pits

One of my favorite button-box treasures is a delicate, thumbnail-sized basket hand-carved from an apricot pit. Found nestled among the buttons in a box I found at a garage sale, the basket has a handle at the top and different designs on each side, including an anchor on one side and the initial "G" on the other (Fig. 3-13). At first I thought it

3-13

was a shank-type button but later learned that around 1880 sailors with time, good eyesight and patience carved tiny baskets to show off their whittling skills. Perhaps you have one in your button box, too.

Button collectors tell me that people also have carved buttons from peach, apricot, and plum pits. One collector even showed me a button from Israel carved from an olive pit.

Vegetable Ivory

Vegetable ivory is made from the hard fruit of the tagua palm (*phytelephas macrocarpa*), which is native to the equatorial rain forests of South America (Fig. 3-14). Natives have used the substance for fashioning personal items for centuries.

Fig. 3-14 *Vegetable ivory buttons are made from the hard fruit of the tagua palm, native to the South American rain forests.*

The first commercially made vegetable ivory buttons were made in England in the 1840s. The raw materials were imported from Venezuela by a toymaker. At around the same time, vegetable ivory buttons also were manufactured in the United States.

Buttons made from this material may soon become more common. Button factories established in Ecuador will enable residents to support themselves without clearing the forests for farming. Several major U.S. clothing manufacturers have agreed to purchase the buttons.

Odd Fact

In the film The Cocoanuts *(1929), Harpo Marx ate the buttons off a bellman's vest. They were made of licorice.*

Wood

Buttons have been made from nearly every type of
wood since the eighteenth century. The oldest buttons, made from hardwoods such as apple, boxwood,
or yew, were very simple. Nineteenth-century wooden
buttons, on the other hand, often were elaborately
carved and/or painted. It's difficult to identify the
specific woods used to make these buttons without
cutting into them.

Wood was used for many of the buttons made
during World War II, when other materials such as
bone, shell, and metal were in short supply.

Philadelphia buttonmaker Benjamin Randolph may
have made this country's first wooden buttons by hand
in his small shop around 1770. Some believe that
wooden buttons first were mass-produced in the
United States in the 1840s at a mill owned by Williston
Thayer in Williamsburg, Massachusetts. Wooden
buttons also were manufactured around the same time
at Healy's Mill in West Chesterfield, Massachusetts
(Fig. 3-15).

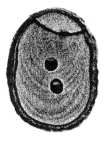

Fig. 3-15 *The Healy Shop
in West Chesterfield,
Massachusetts, produced
wooden buttons in the
mid-19th century. The
building burned in 1920.
Photograph courtesy of
Peter Banister.*

4. Buttons on Clothing

  History

Ordinary Buttons on Ordinary Clothing

If you were a peasant in the Middle Ages, getting dressed involved putting on a homespun tunic, some sort of leg covering and, if it was cold outside, a cloak. It's likely that these garments closed with lacing or hooks rather than with buttons. The first buttons probably were purely ornamental and seen only on the clothing of rich people. The word "button" comes from the French *bouton* (the root of which is *bouter*, to push). The first buttonhole is believed to have appeared after the button, sometime during the thirteenth century, but no one really knows for sure.

Buttons first gained real importance during the Renaissance, when rich men wore jeweled buttons on their elegant clothing. Women's gowns were sometimes made with sets of sleeves that buttoned on and off. But the mostly handcrafted buttons were still too expensive for common people. Not until the eighteenth century, when new machinery and cheaper materials were introduced, did buttons become affordable.

Clothing styles changed as people were influenced by the clothing worn by invaders, travelers to other lands, and popular rulers. Buttons began to be used decoratively and functionally. For example, the use of buttons as a decorative element in India was, according to scholar S. N. Dar, "perhaps originally a result of Muslim influence" on the country. The idea of using buttons as fasteners probably was introduced later by European visitors.

In cultures throughout the world, common people made special outfits to be worn only on Sundays and/or at festivals. These outfits were embellished with special touches, such as embroidery or special buttons, and handed down from generation to generation.

The U.S.S.R. has perhaps the richest tradition of button-embellished clothing. Buttons appear on the festival costumes of many people living near trade routes. We can safely guess that the buttons were obtained from traders traveling these routes and that the buttons were prized like jewelry. People in the following provinces traditionally wore button-embellished clothing on special occasions: Ryazan (Fig. 4-1), Tula (Fig. 4-2), Voronezh (Fig. 4-3), and Semipalatinsk (Fig. 4-4). Many of the

Detail
red thread
on white
button

← BUTTONS

Women's back
adornment
Late 19th - early 20th
century
Ryazan province
U.S.S.R.

4-1

Rosettes
with
Buttons

Some
with long
ribbons

Young woman's festival
dress ; Tula Province
U.S.S.R - Mid-19th century
4-2

Sash from
bridegroom's
costume
Late 19th
century

← Red

Beads
Green
Button in
center
← Red
Green

Voronezh Province
U.S.S.R.

4-3

← Red and black
Print fabric
← Pink
Buttons
on black
ribbon
← Yellow, green, and
red Fringe

Hem of dress
early 20th century
Voronezh Province
U.S.S.R.

green and
yellow yarn
Fringe

Mid-19th century
Semipalatinsk province
U.S.S.R.

Red →
BUTTON-EMBELLISHED
TOP HAT
4-4

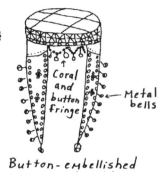

Button-embellished
Women's headdress
c. 1930
Kirghiz S.S.R.
4-5

peoples of Siberia wore garments that included button ornamentation, including the nomadic Kirghiz, whose women still wear a headdress decorated with coral and mother-of-pearl buttons (Fig. 4-5).

Other examples of traditional festival costumes with special buttons include:

The burghers of Friesland in the northern part of the Netherlands wore black jackets and brocade waistcoats embellished with silver buttons to show off their wealth.

Bavarian men (circa 1857) wore brightly colored vests and jackets embellished with plenty of buttons (Fig. 4-6).

Fig. 4-6 Traditional folk costumes from Bavaria. Antique postcard from the author's collection.

Silver button
and trinket
embellished festival
dress from
Laesø, Denmark
4-7

Betrothed women on the Danish island of Laesø would travel many miles to obtain silver jewelry and buttons for their weddings. This journey was called "fetching silver." Only married women were allowed to wear the precious metal (Fig. 4-7).

Men in Viana do Castello in the Minho district of Portugal wear a traditional festival costume featuring a short black jacket lined in red with silver buttons sewn in curves (Fig. 4-8).

The traditional male folk costume of Turégano in the Segovia region of Spain features gold and silver buttons that dangle from a long thread shank (Fig. 4-9). Similar tasslelike buttons are found on men's vests in Majorca (Fig. 4-10).

But much of the story of buttons lies in ordinary buttons, many of which have been used in extraordinary ways. Many cultures, particularly nomadic ones, admire buttons so much that they are used as a major decorative element on everyday clothing. Most cultures continue to use buttons both as fasteners and for nonfunctional ornamentation.

In India, for example, buttons have continued to serve two purposes. In the eighteenth century, stylish men of the Punjab wore tight, black alpaca waistcoats "displaying several rows of mother-of-pearl buttons all around the collar with quite a grotesque effect." Scholar S. N. Dar continues, "Gold and silver buttons are still commonly worn by those who like to be foppishly dressed."

In addition to the Kirghiz (mentioned previously), the women of several other nomadic groups wear headdresses studded with small white buttons. The Rashaida women of Eastern Sudan wear veils (*burdas*) embellished with buttons, silver thread, and metal pendants (Fig. 4-11). *Burdas* are removed only in extreme privacy.

Men's black jacket

Silver buttons are always sewn in a curve
Viana do Castello (Minho district), Portugal   4-8

Red Lining

Thread

Dangling Shank button

FABRIC

Gold and silver buttons were worn by Men in Turégano (Segovia region), Spain.   4-9

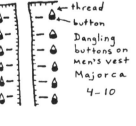

thread
button
Dangling buttons on Men's vest Majorca   4-10

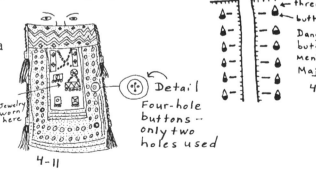

Jewelry worn here

4-11

Detail
Four-hole buttons -- only two holes used

The women of eastern Afghanistan (Koristan and Nuristan) wear voluminous cotton dresses elaborately embellished with embroidery, silver beads, red glass, and mother-of-pearl buttons (plates 7A and 7B). The head always is covered with a shawl or *chadar*, also embroidered and decorated with beads, shells, snaps, zippers, and buttons.

According to Palestinian costume expert Shelagh Weir, Bedouin women have embellished their clothing with buttons (mother-of-pearl and/or metal military buttons) for years. Southern Bedouin women wear a headdress called a *wuga*, which features coral, stones, beads, cowrie shells, and buttons (Fig. 4-12).

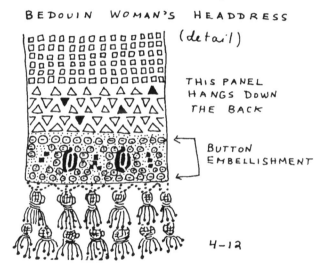

BEDOUIN WOMAN'S HEADDRESS

(detail)

THIS PANEL HANGS DOWN THE BACK

BUTTON EMBELLISHMENT

4-12

4-13 MASAI child's headdress

BUTTONS

In Arabia, Hejazi women wear a hood embellished with cowrie shells, silk tassels, and mother-of-pearl buttons (plate 5).

Finally, the Masai of Kenya wear multicolored beaded jewelry studded here and there with mother-of-pearl and other handcrafted buttons (Fig. 4-13).

London's Pearly Kings and Queens

Perhaps the most well-known button-encrusted clothing is worn by London's Pearly Kings and Queens (Fig. 4-14). The tradition originated in the nineteenth

Fig. 4-14 George and Rose Matthews Smith, Pearly King and Queen of Camden, collecting for charity in Trafalgar Square, London. Mrs. Smith, whose parents were the first Pearly couple, first wore buttons when she was eighteen months old. Photograph courtesy of the British Tourist Authority.

century in London's East End. In 1834 Charles Dickens mentioned the pearl buttons on clothing worn by the cockney costermongers who sold fruit and vegetables on London's streets (Fig. 4-15).

Boys Apples buy. Jocky looks shy

Fig. 4-15 Pearly Kings and Queens are descendants of London's costermongers who sold fruit, vegetables, and household goods at street markets. Illustration from the Dover Pictorial Archive Series.

It wasn't until 1880, however, that Henry Croft, a cockney roadsweeper, invented the first button-encrusted Pearly costume. Croft, who was less than five feet tall, felt the need to draw attention to himself when collecting money for the poor at carnivals. He decorated a heavy brown wool suit with smoked pearl buttons so that people would notice him.

There are conflicting stories about how other cockneys obtained enough pearl buttons to copy Croft's outfit. Some say that a Japanese cargo ship lost its cargo of pearl buttons in the Thames and the cargo washed ashore, where it was claimed by scavengers. Others claim that the ship and cargo were seized for tax evasion and the

buttons were sold at bargain prices.

Pearly Kings and Queens began collecting

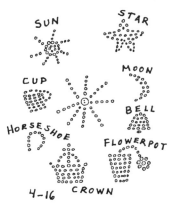

4-16

money for the poor at charity events throughout London's East End. At first the cloth was completely covered with pearl buttons. Sixty thousand were required for a single suit, which took at least three months to make. Suits were sewn by both men and women.

Soon people developed individual patterns, borders, and symbols to distinguish their outfits

(Fig. 4-16). It was considered bad form to copy another's pattern. Bill Davidson, Pearly King of West Ham, even made an outfit for his dog, Rover. Rover wore a special button-encrusted blanket and cap and barked, "thank you," for contributions.

Pearly outfits are handed down from generation to generation. Some of the early garments are still worn today. Pearly royalty is declining in numbers, but a few still work London's street markets, raising money for disabled children, the elderly, and other unfortunates.

The original Pearly King, Henry Croft, is buried at London's Finchley cemetery. His tomb features a statue of him wearing his button suit.

Button Use by
Pacific Northwest Coast Indians

In the late 1700s and early 1800s, Pacific Northwest Coast Indians (Gitksan, Haida, Heiltsuk, Kwagiutl, Nishga, Tahltan/Tlingit, Tsimshian, and others) often traded furs for woolen blankets from the Hudson Bay Company. The blankets were made into highly valued robes used for ceremonial purposes. According to scholars Doreen Jensen and Polly Sargent, "The robe's specific role varies from area to area, village to village, house to house, and even from chief to chief in the same house."[3]

No one is sure who made the first button blanket. Kwagiutl legend traces it to a member of the tribe who saw a cockney Pearly King and liked what he saw. Others claim that the first button blanketmaker was inspired by the rows of white pearl buttons on the uniform of a British sailor.

Early photographs, however, indicate that the Indians first decorated the blankets with feathers and abalone shell. These materials eventually were replaced by pearl buttons obtained from Spanish, English, and Russian traders. The buttons

Fig. 4-17 *This stitchery by the author was inspired by Pacific Northwest Indian button blankets. It features colored felt, buttons, and beads.*

often came from sailors' uniforms and saved the Indians time because holes were already drilled in the shell. A Gitksan explained: "Good mother-of-pearl buttons

are a thousand times easier to use, and besides, they shine so nicely."

The blankets usually are dark blue with red flannel appliqué outlined with pearl buttons; the design depicts a family's personal symbol or crest (plate 6). Popular symbols include the frog, raven, whale, and thunderbird. Dempsey Bob, a contemporary artist of Tahltan/Tlingit descent, says, "When we wear our blankets, we show our face. We show who we are and where we come from" (Fig. 4-17).

In the Gitksan language, the blankets are called *gwiss gan m'ala*, which translates to "covering [or robe] with buttons." The ceremonial robes are worn over the shoulders like cloaks.

The Indians traditionally decorated flannel and woolen shirts, leggings, and aprons in the same manner. Both robes and

clothing are handed down from one generation to the next.

Athapascan Indians (Ahtena and Tanana), living in the far north at the turn of the century (circa 1902), also utilized buttons obtained from traders to embellish their clothing (Fig. 4-18).

Button blankets were not made as often after 1880 because the Indians were discouraged from participating in traditional ceremonies. Blanketmaking resumed in the 1950s, however. Button blankets are currently made at the Southeast Alaska Indian Cultural Center in the Sitka Visitor's Center at Sitka National Historical Park, Sitka, Alaska (Fig. 4-19). Classes in bead and button work are often offered. For information, contact the center at P.O. Box 944, Sitka, AK 99835. The telephone number is (907) 747-8061.

Fig. 4-18 *Group of Athapascan women and children (Upper Ahtena or Upper Tanana). The hat of the boy in the foreground and the dress on the girl at the left are decorated with bone buttons, probably obtained from traders along the Yukon River. Photograph by the Miles Brothers, summer 1920. Photograph courtesy of the Smithsonian Institution (photo number: 56,715).*

Fig. 4-19 *Ester Littlefield, instructor in the Heritage Department, Sitka National Historical Park, working on a traditional Tlingit button blanket. Photograph courtesy of Sitka National Historical Park.*

Button Use by Modern Designers

In the early 1970s British designer Zandra Rhodes, inspired by a visit to a London button manufacturer, scattered button-centered flowers on a printed fabric she named Button Flower. She later studied buttons and bows in the Costume Court of the Victoria and Albert Museum and incorporated more buttons into her collection. Her first London fashion show also featured button jewelry by artist Mick Milligan.

Mississippi-born, Paris-based designer Patrick Kelly (1954–1990) is usually credited with inspiring the current button mania. His first creations were made with a borrowed sewing machine and sold at the Paris flea market and on the street near Saint-Germain-des-Prés. Kelly, who referred to himself as "the black male version of Lucille Ball,"[4] began showing his designs in 1985 at fashion shows featuring exuberant, foot-tapping music. "I design for fat women, skinny women, all kinds of women. My message is, 'You're beautiful just the way you are,'"[5] said Kelly in a 1987 interview with *People Weekly* reporter Bonnie Johnson.

Kelly's clothes were always lighthearted and fun; many featured numerous colorful buttons (Fig. 4-20). He made his first "button dress" in 1982, using a bolt of cotton jersey purchased at the Paris flea market. He once claimed that the inspiration for the jumble of buttons came from buttons sewn on his childhood sweaters by his grandmother, who rarely used two that matched.

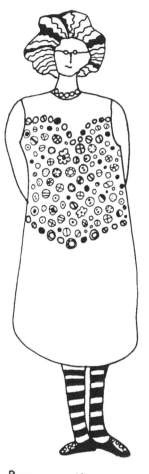

BUTTON HEART
DRESS
by PATRICK KELLY
4-20

Other designers have followed his lead. For example, Franco Moschino's clothing features heart-shaped buttons, as well as giant buttons and buttonholes. Christian Francis Roth's 1989 spring collection featured a "breakfast suit" with eggs that had yellow button yolks (Fig. 4-21) and his "elevator jacket" had numbered buttons (and one marked "Lobby").

But you don't have to buy designer clothes to effect the Patrick Kelly look. Today, Kelly-inspired designs are found in pattern books and department stores. Burda, the German pattern company, featured a Kelly-inspired button jacket in its spring 1990 pattern collection (plate 10). California-based shoe company New York Transit markets button-encrusted shoes (Fig. 4-22).

Using a curved needle and heavy-duty thread, I covered a young friend's sneakers with buttons (see back cover). I think Patrick Kelly would approve.

Fig. 4-21 Christian Francis Roth's "breakfast suit" features eggs sunny-side-up; the yolks are buttons. Roth has been called the "Schiaparelli of the 90s." Photograph courtesy of Christian Francis Roth.

Fig. 4-22 The Hayward, California-based shoe manufacturer New York Transit featured button-encrusted flats in a recent collection.

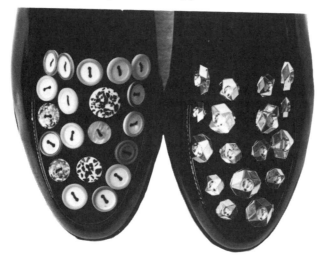

Creating

5. Making Your Own Buttons

The Button Lover's Book

You have looked all over town for buttons to match the beautiful silk fabric you found in China, but your search has been unsuccessful. Don't put the fabric away. Consider making your own buttons. Handmade buttons are often better than store-bought buttons. You can mix the perfect color, and buttons you make yourself are bound to be unique.

Buttons can be made from many materials. The ones I've tried are discussed in this chapter. Use your imagination; perhaps you can think of other buttonmaking materials.

In case you're not familiar with some of the ingredients or tools I mention, here's some information in alphabetical order to help you locate them:

Antler is not something most of us have at our fingertips. Consult Other Button Resources in the Appendices to learn where to buy it.

Button-covering kits (William Prym, Singer, and Maxant are common brands) are available in fabric stores and by mail. Consult Other Button Resources in the Appendices for mail-order sources.

Small **cookie** or **aspic cutters** are available in cooking shops or by mail. Consult Other Button Resources in the Appendices for mail-order suppliers.

A **coping saw** has a blade mounted in a U-shaped frame. The saw is commonly used for cutting intricate patterns in wood. You can buy one at a hardware store.

Cyanoacrylate (Super Glue) is a permanent bonding glue. Buy it at hardware stores or at some drugstores. Check the tube for the word "cyanoacrylate."

Game pieces for use as buttons are best found at garage or rummage sales. You often can buy a boxed game for a quarter. I usually toss everything but the game pieces. You can also order game pieces by mail. Consult Other Button Resources in the Appendices for mail-order sources.

Needle-nosed jeweler's files are available at jewelers' supply stores or by mail. Consult Other Button Resources in the Appendices for mail-order sources.

Needle-nosed pliers are available in hardware stores, jewelers' supply stores, and by mail. Consult Other Button Resources in the Appendices for mail-order sources.

Plasticine clay is ordinary children's clay. It's available at toy stores and dime stores.

Antler Buttons

If you can find some antlers, it's easy to make them into buttons. Antler buttons are especially handsome on handwoven fabrics.

Materials

Deer antlers or the tips of elk antlers
Coping saw
Pen or pencil
Drill and drill bit
Plasticine clay
Sandpaper
Mineral oil (optional)

How to Do It

1. Saw antler with a coping saw into button-sized sections and mark the placement of the holes with a pen or pencil (Fig. 5-1).

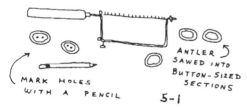

ANTLER SAWED INTO BUTTON-SIZED SECTIONS

MARK HOLES WITH A PENCIL

5-1

2. Set the sections on a piece of plasticine clay to hold them steady. Drill the holes (Fig. 5-2)

ANTLER SECTIONS WITH HOLES

LUMP OF PLASTICINE CLAY HOLDS BUTTON STEADY FOR DRILLING

5-2

3. Smooth the rough edges with sandpaper.

4. Rub with a small amount of mineral oil. Excess oil should soak into the antler. Before sewing the buttons to a garment, rub them carefully with a clean cloth to remove any traces of oil.

Avocado Pit Buttons

California artist Ann deWitt taught me how to make buttons out of avocado pits. She says they're a reasonable substitute for vegetable ivory and I agree. Besides, making avocado pit buttons is a good excuse for a guacamole party.

Materials

Fresh avocado pits (Fig. 5-3)

Coping saw

Linoleum cutting tools

Pen or pencil

Plasticine clay

Drill and drill bits (size depends on how large you want the holes)

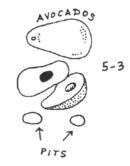

AVOCADOS

5-3

PITS

How to Do It

1. Split the pits in half and slice button-sized sections with a coping saw (Fig. 5-4), or carve the halves into interesting button shapes. Mark the holes with a pen or pencil.

PITS

HALVE the PIT

SAW ON DOTTED LINE

MARK HOLES WITH A PENCIL

BUTTON BLANKS

5-4

2. Set button shapes on a piece of plasticine clay to hold them steady. Drill the holes. If you like, carve textures into the buttons with linoleum cutting tools (Fig. 5-5).

LUMP OF PLASTICINE CLAY HOLDS BUTTON STEADY

DRILL HOLES

5-5

carve textures if you like

LINOLEUM CUTTING TOOLS

5-5

3. Set the buttons in a cool place for three to four weeks to dry. The pits become very hard and mottled in color.

Bone Buttons

Wait! Don't give that bone to Bowser. Keep it for yourself and make buttons. I've had the best luck with beef and lamb bones (leg bones are best). I usually use the bone to make soup first, as simmering removes most of the meat.

Chicken and turkey bones don't make great buttons. They are brittle and tend to shatter.

Materials

Assorted bones

Coping saw

Pen or pencil

Plasticine clay

Drill and drill bit

Glass or enamel cooking pot

Stove

Baking soda

Powdered alum (found in the spice section at the grocery store)

Water

Sandpaper and assorted files

How to Do It

1. Remove meat from the bone.

2. Cut rough button shapes with a coping saw.

3. Boil the button pieces in a covered glass or enamel pot for one hour in a solution of baking soda, powdered alum, and water (Fig. 5-6). I use about 1/2 cup of baking soda and one teaspoon of alum to two quarts of water, but the proportions need not be exact. Be sure to watch the pot, so it won't boil dry. And open some windows; it won't smell like roses.

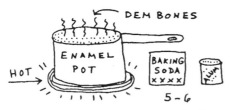

5-6

4. Set the bone in the sun to dry for several days, or soak it for two days in equal amounts of bleach and water (Fig. 5-7).

5. You can make bone buttons look older and darker by antiquing them. Here's how: After drying the button shapes in the sun, sand them lightly with medium-weight sandpaper to open the grain. Then sauté them in salted corn oil, stirring until the bone is a bit darker than you want. The color will lighten when the bone dries. Remove buttons from oil and wipe off excess with a paper towel.

6. If you want colored buttons, you can dye them by boiling them for an hour in an all-purpose household dye, such as Rit or Tintex.

7. Mark the holes and set the shapes on a piece of plasticine clay to hold them steady. Drill the holes and smooth the button shapes with sandpaper and files.

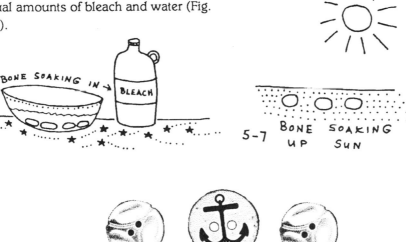

Ceramic Buttons

Ceramic buttons are special because they've never been produced in the same mass quantities as those made of plastic, metal, and mother-of-pearl.

Since most of us don't have the materials to work with clay at home, here are recipes for two types of ceramiclike buttons that can be made without a kiln.

Acrylic Modeling Compound Buttons

Acrylic modeling compound is a synthetic plastic material available at many all-purpose craft shops or by mail (consult Other Button Resources in the Appendices). Eberhard Faber's FIMO and Polyform Products' Sculpey III and PRO MAT II are popular brands. The modeling compound hardens when baked in a conventional oven. The hardened material is very durable and is excellent for buttons. It comes in many colors, so you can make custom-designed buttons to match a special fabric or to jazz up an outdated dress.

Acrylic modeling compound is appropriate for use with children. It's quite expensive, however. Baker's clay, discussed later, is a less expensive alternative for buttons.

Materials

Acrylic modeling compound

Rolling pin (plastic is better because the modeling compound tends to stick to wood) or smooth glass jar

Smooth cutting board or glass plate

Pointed tool for piercing the holes and/or creating textures on the buttons (metal skewer or knitting needle)

Small aspic and cookie cutters for cutting the buttons from the modeling compound

Spatula and/or knife

Beads, rhinestones, and other embellishments

Tweezers for placing embellishments on the buttons

Cookie sheet or piece of aluminum foil

Conventional or toaster oven (not microwave)

Protective lacquer and paintbrush (optional)

Cyanoacrylate (Super Glue) or epoxy

How to Do It

1. Preheat the oven. Consult the instructions that came with your modeling compound for the recommended temperature for that brand.

2. In order to become pliable, acrylic modeling compound must be worked and kneaded in the warmth of your hands (Fig. 5-8).

knead the dough

5-8

Kneading will take less time if you set the modeling compound outside in the sun or on a heating pad to warm it first (Fig. 5-9). Wash your hands before you

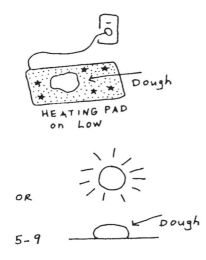

HEATING PAD
on LOW

OR

5-9

Dough

Dough

begin (and each time you switch colors) because light-colored modeling compounds can pick up dirt and begin to look dingy. PRO MAT II is best warmed by putting it in a plastic bag and immersing it in warm water for a few minutes until it becomes workable (Fig. 5-10).

Warm
Water

Dough in
Plastic bag   5-10

3. Once the modeling compound is warm and well kneaded, roll it out with

a rolling pin or glass jar, as you do with cookie dough (Fig. 5-11). Buttons for

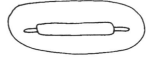

ROLL OUT WITH
5-11   A ROLLING PIN

delicate garments should be at least 1/8" thick. If the buttons are for a garment that will get lots of wear, however, make them thicker (1/4").

4. Buttons made with acrylic modeling compound can be made in solid colors, or you can marbleize two or three colors of modeling compound together. To combine colors:

(a) Roll a 1/2"-thick "snake" for each color (Fig. 5-12).

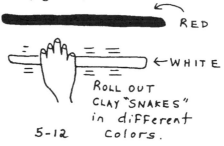

RED

WHITE

ROLL OUT
CLAY "SNAKES"
in different
5-12   colors.

(b) Twist the different colored "snakes" together like a candy cane (Fig. 5-13).

TWIST TWO "SNAKES"
TOGETHER LIKE A
CANDY CANE   5-13

(c) Roll this twist on your cutting board to make a two-color "snake" (Fig. 5-14). Add a third color by making another colored "snake" and combining it with your two-color "snake" and by repeating steps (b) and (c) (Fig. 5-15).

ROLL THE CANDY CANE
5-14 to COMBINE COLORS

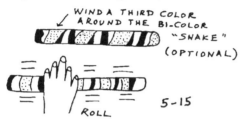

WIND A THIRD COLOR AROUND THE BI-COLOR "SNAKE" (OPTIONAL)

5-15

ROLL

Mix new colors by continuing to fold and twist the modeling material until the colors are throughly blended. You can either roll out the snake like cookie dough (as explained above) and proceed with the next step, or slice button-sized slices from the multicolored roll with a knife and skip to decorating the buttons.

5. Cut shapes with small aspic or cookie cutters or bottle caps (Fig. 5-16). If you don't have cookie cutters, make paper patterns to cut around or cut shapes freehand with a knife (Fig. 5-17).

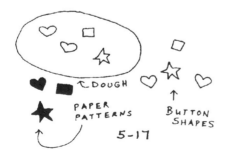

DOUGH
PAPER PATTERNS
BUTTON SHAPES
5-17

Fig. 5-16 You often can find small cookie cutters at kitchen supply shops. They can be used to make whimsical buttons that are fun on children's clothing.

You can improve "ugly duckling buttons" by molding acrylic modeling compound over them. Metal buttons make the best bases as most can tolerate the brief oven baking. To update an old button, roll clay to 1/8" thick and mold it securely, overlapping the edges of the base button (Fig. 5-18).

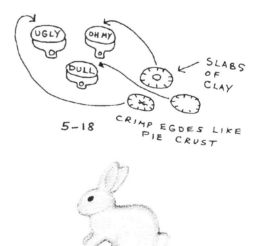

UGLY   OH MY
DULL
SLABS OF CLAY
5-18
CRIMP EDGES LIKE PIE CRUST

6. Decorate buttons by pressing beads, rhinestones or other embellishments into the soft clay (Figs. 5-19 and 5-20).

ADD BEADS
and other SPARKLES

TWEEZERS
5-19

Fig. 5-20 *Use tweezers to place beads and other embellishments on the soft buttons.*

These embellishments should withstand baking and will usually adhere to the clay without glue. Check them after baking and secure loose stones or beads with cyanoacrylate or epoxy.

7. For holes, pierce each button with a metal skewer or knitting needle before baking (Fig. 5-21), or drill holes after the

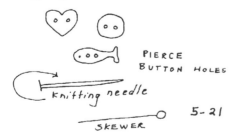

PIERCE
BUTTON HOLES

knitting needle

5-21

SKEWER

clay is baked. An alternative is a shank hole constructed with modeling compound on the back of the button (Fig. 5-22).

CONSTRUCT MOLDED
SHANKS WITH
CLAY
5-22

8. Move shapes from the rolling/cutting surface to a cookie sheet or piece of aluminum foil for baking. Arrange buttons so they don't touch one another (Fig. 5-23). Acrylic modeling compounds do not change size during baking, so you don't have to allow for expansion.

BAKE
SHANK
BUTTONS
UPSIDE
DOWN

BUTTONS READY
FOR BAKING ON
COOKIE SHEET
5-23

9. Baking times will vary according to the thickness of the buttons and the manufacturer's instructions. A good rule of thumb is 20 to 30 minutes per half inch of thickness. Consult the

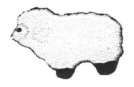

manufacturer's instructions for your specific modeling compound. In my experience, half the suggested baking time has been sufficient for baking buttons. Acrylic modeling compounds will scorch when overbaked. If you smell the baking clay (the odor of melting plastic), remove the buttons from the oven immediately.

10. Remove the buttons from the oven to cool. If the buttons are hard to remove from the cookie sheet, your oven is too hot.

11. When the buttons have cooled, textures can be carved into the modeling material (Fig. 5-24). Buttons can be finished with a coat of

protective lacquer (use that suggested by the manufacturer of your modeling compound) (Fig. 5-25) or left plain. The lacquer makes the buttons shiny

and adds a little extra protection. Unlacquered buttons can become soiled. Should you decide you don't like the color of your buttons, they can be painted over with acrylic paint and sealed with acrylic glaze.

12. Store unused modeling materials (for up to two years) in foil or in an airtight tin until your next buttonmaking session. Do not store the modeling material in containers made of plastic foam. (Fig. 5-26 shows finished buttons.)

Fig. 5-26 *Last time I made these buttons from acrylic modeling compound, I placed them in a bowl on the kitchen counter. When friends arrived for supper one guest thought they were for eating. When I told her they were buttons she exclaimed, "I just love coming to your house! We never know what we're going to see next."*

Baker's Clay Buttons

Make similar and less expensive buttons from baker's clay. You probably already have the ingredients in your kitchen. Baker's clay buttons are a bit less durable than those made with acrylic modeling compound. However, they'll hold up if coated with lacquer and treated with care. This is a fun rainy day project for children.

Materials

4 cups all-purpose flour

1 cup salt

1-1/2 cups water

Mixing bowl

Rolling pin or smooth glass jar

Smooth cutting board or glass plate

Pointed tool for piercing holes and/or creating textures on the buttons (metal skewer or knitting needle)

Small aspic and cookie cutters for cutting buttons from the modeling compound

Spatula and/or knife

Beads, rhinestones, and other embellishments

Tweezers for placing embellishments on the buttons

Cookie sheet or piece of aluminum foil

Conventional or toaster oven (not microwave)

Protective lacquer (and/or enamel paints, paintbrushes, and paint thinner)

Toothpicks

Two bricks or shoe boxes

Cyanoacrylate (Super Glue) or epoxy

How to Do It

1. Preheat the oven to 350° F (Fig. 5-27).

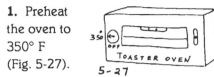

5-27

2. Combine flour and salt and mix well (Fig. 5-28). Add the water all at once and stir well (Fig. 5-29).

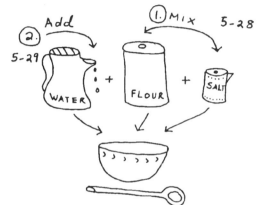

3. Turn out onto a lightly floured surface and knead for five minutes. The baker's clay is ready to use when it has a velvety texture. Wash the mixing bowl immediately because hardened dough is difficult to remove.

4. Roll dough on a flat, smooth, floured surface to 1/8" to 1/4" thick (Fig. 5-30).

5-30 ROLL DOUGH WITH ROLLING PIN

54

*The
Button
Lover's
Book*

Odd Fact

According to Faith McNulty, Beatrix Potter tore a button off a coat as an excuse to go into a tailor's shop to sketch the tailor at work "surrounded by the oddments of his craft." The results of Potter's ruse appear in her book The Tailor of Gloucester.[6]

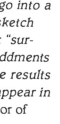

Cut shapes with small aspic or cookie cutters or bottle caps (Fig. 5-31). If you don't have cookie cutters, make paper patterns to cut around or cut shapes freehand with a knife.

5. Decorate buttons by pressing beads, rhinestones, or

other embellishments into the soft clay (Fig. 5-32). These embellishments should withstand baking and will usually adhere to the clay without glue.

Check them after baking and secure loose stones or beads with cyanoacrylate or epoxy.

6. For holes, pierce the buttons with a metal skewer or knitting needle before baking (Fig. 5-33). I do not recommend making shank-type buttons out of baker's clay.

PIERCE BUTTON HOLES and create textures

5-33

7. Bake buttons on a cookie sheet (Fig. 5-34) for approximately ten minutes. Watch them. As with cookies, the longer they bake, the darker they get. Color possibilities range from sandy brown to black.

BAKE ON COOKIE SHEET 5-34

8. Coat the buttons with protective lacquer to protect them in laundering. If you don't like the natural cookie

Plate 6 *(Above) Tlingit button blanket, late nineteenth century, from the Walter Walters Collection, Thomas Burke Memorial Washington State Museum, Seattle, Washington. The blanket depicts the frog crest of the Tlingit Raven clan in mother-of-pearl buttons on dark blue and red flannel. Photograph courtesy of the Thomas Burke Memorial Washington State Museum. (Catalog number: 1-1495)*

Plate 5 *(Overleaf) Hijazi tribeswoman's garment embellished with mother-of-pearl buttons, cowrie shells, silk tassels, and fabric appliqués. Photograph by Paul Rocheleau. Courtesy of Johara Alatas.*

Plate 7A (left) Detail of Plate 7B.

Plate 7B (below) Woman's ceremonial dress from Nouristan, Afghanistan, circa early to mid-nineteenth century. Handwoven black cotton plain weave ground—beaded, lined, and embroidered— is used in the bodice and sleeves. The skirt consists of woven triangles pieced together from the waistline. The upper part of the dress has geometric decorations of polychrome embroidery, beading, applied bands of shell and plastic buttons, and metallic implements. Sleeve edges feature hammered metallic beads. Ruth Lincoln Fisher Fund. Photograph courtesy of the Textile Museum, Washington, D.C. (Accession number: 1984.22.1)

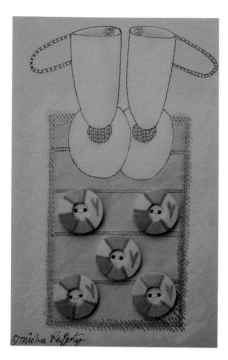

Plate 8A (left) British artist Trisha Rafferty makes unique sets of porcelain buttons and mounts them on hand-colored cards. Her buttons are so special that many collectors frame them rather than using them on clothing. Rafferty's address is listed in the Mail-Order Sources for Buttons listing in the Appendices.

Plate 8B (below) Detail of Mexican Motifs (6' wide by 4' high) by Fran Patterson of Austin, Texas, 1986. The artist used colorful felt, cotton, buttons, and ribbon to make this large wall piece for a Mexican restaurant. Photograph courtesy of the artist.

look (Fig. 5-35), baker's clay buttons can be painted instead with colored enamels (Fig. 5-36). A button will be easier to handle during this process if you insert a toothpick

5-36

through one of the holes (Fig. 5-37). Hold the toothpick while you paint both sides of the button. Then suspend the toothpick

HOLD ON SKEWER WHILE
5-37 PAINTING

between two bricks or shoe boxes until the paint is dry (Fig. 5-38). After the paint is dry, check the insides of the holes to be sure the baker's clay is completely covered with paint. Then, if necessary, add additional paint. (Fig. 5-39 shows finished buttons.)

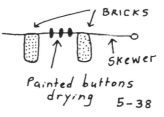

BRICKS
SKEWER
Painted buttons drying 5-38

Fig. 5-39 *The painted buttons are shiny and cheerful.*

Covered Buttons

Luckily it no longer takes nine years to learn how to cover buttons. Button-covering kits are widely available and make the procedure super easy.

Covered buttons are appropriate for almost every type of garment. They can provide a polished, coordinated look. They are especially fun for dressy clothes because the buttons can be embellished with

elegant embroidery, pearls, beads, sequins, or jewels (plate 11B).

You can also use button-covering kits to make covered buttons for upholstered furniture or pillows.

Fabric-Covered Buttons Using Kits

Materials

Button-covering kit (William Prym, Singer, and Maxant are common brands)

Fabric or soft leather

Scissors (for paper and fabric)

"Disappearing" fabric marking pencil

Piece of stiff paper

Embellishments such as beads, pearls, embroidery floss, fabric paints and brushes, sequins, etc.

Spool of thread

Hammer

How to Do It

1. If you're using a print fabric to cover buttons, make a "viewer" (the same size as the button form) out of paper to assist in deciding which part of the fabric to use. Trace the button form on a piece of stiff paper and cut out the circle (Fig. 5-40). Now move the paper

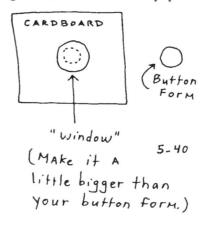

window across the print fabric until you find a pleasing design (Fig. 5-41). Be

MOVE WINDOW UNTIL YOU LIKE WHAT YOU SEE.

5-41 FABRIC

sure to consider both sides of the fabric; sometimes the wrong side is better. If using leather to cover buttons, consider both sides of the skin. As with fabric, sometimes the wrong side is more attractive. When you find a portion of the fabric that you like, trace around the paper window with a fabric marking pencil (Fig. 5-42).

TRACE AROUND Window with A Pencil
5-42

2. Now hold the fabric against the metal button form to determine if your covered button needs a lining (Fig. 5-43). Linings

5-43 Metal button Form shows through

no lining needed here!

needs lining!

are often necessary for lightweight, sheer, or loosely woven fabrics; otherwise the metal button shell will show. If the fabric is not too bulky or not a print design that shows through the top fabric, you can simply use two layers.

3. Cut the fabric according to the directions that came with your button-covering kit. Different kits recommend different seam allowances.

If using leather, buff the skin (on the side that won't show) with sandpaper before cutting. Buffing makes the skin more pliable and easier to cut.

4. Embellish the fabric with embroidery, beads, sequins, or pearls before covering the button forms (Fig. 5-44).

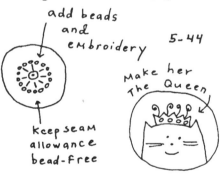

add beads and embroidery   5-44

Make her the Queen

keep seam allowance bead-free

Fabric can also be stenciled or painted freehand with fabric paints (Fig. 5-45).

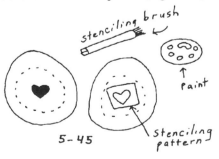

stenciling brush

paint

5-45   stenciling pattern

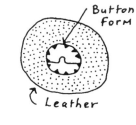

Button
Form

Leather

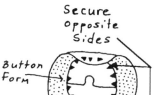

Secure
opposite
Sides

Button
Form

Leather

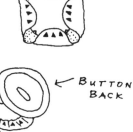

← BUTTON
BACK

↑
BUTTON
FRONT

5-47

5. If your fabric is washable, dampen it before using it to cover buttons (Fig. 5-46). The dampness will make the fabric easier to shape and it will dry to a smooth, tight finish.

5-46

6. Follow the covering instructions that came with your button covering kit.

For leather buttons, lay the leather circle wrong-side up on a table. Place the button form in the center. Secure the leather by folding over an edge and attaching it to the metal prongs on the metal button form. Attach the opposite edge in the same manner. Working across the diameter of the button, secure the leather on the remaining metal prongs (Fig. 5-47).

7. When you're ready to attach the button backing, protect the button by placing the button shank in the hole in a spool of thread (Fig. 5-48). Now lay the

← Set button
shank in
hole

5-48

button face down on a table and tap the spool firmly with a hammer to secure the backing (Fig. 5-49).

HAMMER

TAP
HERE

BUTTON

5-49

(Figs. 5-50 and 5-51 on the next page show finished covered buttons.)

Figs. 5-50 (left) and **5-51** (below) Imaginative use of fabrics and stitching results in unique covered buttons. Embellish some with tiny beads to add sparkle.

59

Making Your Own Buttons

Fabric Covered Buttons
Using Curtain Rings

Materials

Curtain rings (metal or plastic)

Iron-on tape

Iron and ironing board

Fabric or soft leather

Scissors (for paper and fabric)

"Disappearing" fabric marking pencil

Piece of stiff paper

Embellishments such as beads, pearls, embroidery floss, fabric paints and brushes, sequins, etc.

How to Do It

1. Follow steps one and two (above) in the instructions for making covered buttons with a kit.

2. Cut circles of fabric slightly less than twice the diameter of the curtain rings (Fig. 5-52). If your buttons need lining, also cut circles of the lining fabric. Cut circles of iron-on tape about half the diameter of the curtain rings (Fig. 5-53).

FABRIC CIRCLES

5-52

CURTAIN RINGS

IRON-ON TAPE

5-53

CUT CIRCLES

3. Embellish fabric with embroidery, beads, sequins, or pearls before covering the curtain rings (Fig. 5-54). Fabric

5-54 remember seam allowance

embroider or add beads here

can also be stenciled or painted freehand with fabric paints (Fig. 5-55).

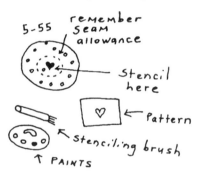

5-55 remember seam allowance

Stencil here

Pattern

Stenciling brush

PAINTS

4. If your fabric is washable, dampen before using it to cover buttons (Fig. 5-56). The dampness will make the

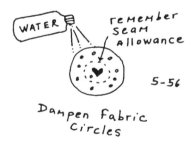

WATER

remember seam allowance

5-56

Dampen Fabric Circles

fabric easier to shape, and it will dry to a smooth, tight finish.

5. Make "sandwiches" out of the fabric and lining circles (with right sides up) (Fig. 5-57).

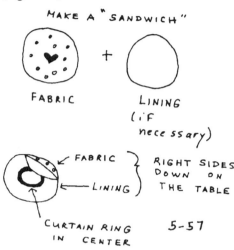

MAKE A "SANDWICH"

FABRIC + LINING (iF necessary)

FABRIC
LINING
} RIGHT SIDES DOWN ON THE TABLE

CURTAIN RING IN CENTER   5-57

6. Sew the "sandwiches" together with a line of running stitches 1/8" from the edge of each circle. If you're not using a lining, you still place a row of running stitches 1/8" from the edge of the circle. When you have finished stitching, don't break off the thread (Fig. 5-58).

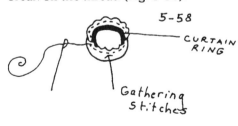

5-58

CURTAIN RING

Gathering Stitches

7. Set a curtain ring in the center of each circle and draw the thread tight, gathering the fabric around the ring (Fig. 5-59). Fasten the fabric with a few

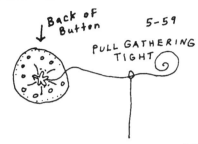

Back oF Button   5-59

PULL GATHERING TIGHT

stitches across the center (Fig. 5-60).

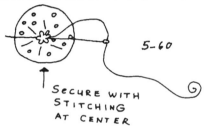

5-60

SECURE WITH STITCHING AT CENTER

Some seamstresses claim that following these last three steps results in smoother kit-made buttons, substituting the metal button form for the curtain ring.

At this point, you also can enhance the shape of the button by stitching around the ring (Fig. 5-61), or poke a

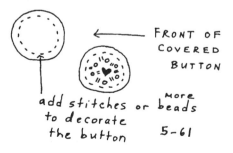

FRONT OF COVERED BUTTON

MORE
add stitches or beads to decorate the button   5-61

hole in the center of the button and insert any metal or solid-colored shank button (Fig. 5-62).

Add slit
And insert
Shank button.

Top View

5-62

8. Affix iron-on tape circles to the back of each button to hide the gathering (Fig. 5-63).

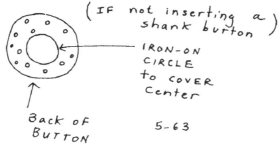

(IF not inserting a
shank button)

IRON-ON
CIRCLE
to COVER
Center

Back of
BUTTON

5-63

Figs. 5-64 *(top)* and **5-65** *(above) Wrap curtain rings with yarn or cord and embellish the center with stitching or fill it with a ball or a knotted button. Photographs by Drew McCalley.*

9. Buttons can also be made by wrapping yarn or cord around the curtain ring and embellishing the center with stitches or inserting a ball or knotted button (Figs. 5-64 and 5-65).

Odd Fact

Time *magazine, November 8, 1948, reported that the children of Mentor, Ohio, requested needles, thread, and buttons instead of candy when trick-or-treating in 1948. They were doing their part to help the people of Suolahti, Finland, a town that Mentor had "adopted."*

TRICK
or
BUTTON

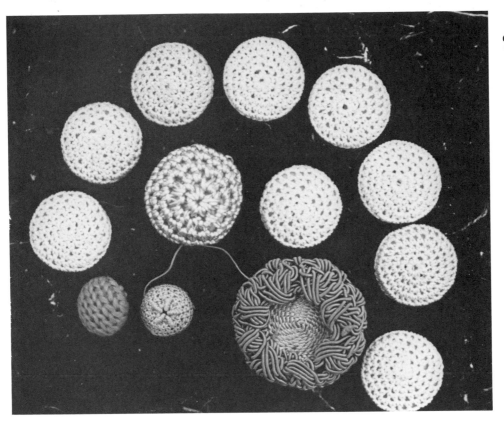

Fig. 5-66 *Crocheted buttons are just the thing for hand-knit sweaters and crocheted garments.*

Crocheted or Knitted Buttons

Buttons for knit and crocheted garments can be handmade from leftover yarn (Fig. 5-66). For fancy buttons, include beads or sequins or embellish with embroidery.

Knit buttons are best made with small needles (size 0-1). You knit a button-sized swatch to use with a button-covering kit or to stitch over a wooden button or metal bottle cap. Wooden buttons work

best as molds because they are less likely to show through the knit fabric.

Simple crocheted buttons are especially easy to make. There are two methods. For a button with a hole in the center, use a curtain ring as a mold. For a solid button, crochet over a wooden button or metal bottle cap. The size of the crochet hook you select depends on the thickness of your yarn. Crochet several swatches using different-sized crochet hooks. Be sure to pull the stitches tight so the mold won't show. Hold the swatches over the curtain ring, wooden button or bottle cap to select a suitable fabric.

Complete instructions for both crocheting and knitting buttons are included in most crochet and knitting manuals. For example, *The Complete Book of Knitting and Crochet* (Marshall Cavendish, London/New York, 1972) has extensive instructions for both types of buttons. *The Reader's Digest Complete Guide to Needlework* (Reader's Digest Association, Inc., Pleasantville, N.Y., 1979) provides instructions for two simple crocheted buttons.

Additional Ideas for Covered Buttons

Insert laminated photographs under clear vinyl fabric, or if you want a "Doris-Day-Photographed-Through-the-Mist" look, place the photo under a sheer fabric such as organdy. Kits for laminating photographs are available at most dime stores (Fig. 5-67).

Insert embroidered badges such as Girl Scout badges or sew-on appliqués under clear vinyl or organdy, or sew them to buttons covered with plain fabric (Fig. 5-68).

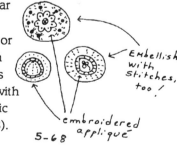

Some button-covering kits feature a metal rim that frames the fabric like a bezel. Consider inserting pennies or quarters, or bits of mirror or metal instead of fabric (Fig. 5-69). A penny is just the right size for a size 36 button. A quarter fits size 45.

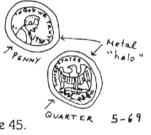

Small cross-stitched medallions make wonderful covered buttons (Fig. 5-70). You can work the cross-stitch by hand or by machine, if yours has such a decorative stitch.

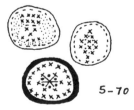

Scraps of embroidered fabric can be used to cover buttons (plate 11B).

For a romantic look, sew lace halos around the rims of your covered buttons (Fig. 5-71).

Make very large buttons (for clown costumes, etc.) by covering lids from orange juice or biscuit dough tins (Fig. 5-73). You can make puffy buttons by inserting a layer of polyester fiberfill.

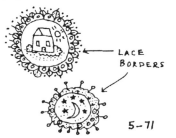

LACE BORDERS

5-71

Make a dust ruffle for your bed. Then use the same fabric to cover large buttons to use on a matching or contrasting comforter (Fig. 5-72).

ORANGE JUICE

BIGGIE BRAND ★ BISCUITS

METAL LID FOR BUTTONS

FIBERFILL

COVER BUTTONS WITH FABRIC AND STUFF WITH FIBERFILL

5-73

BE A CLOWN!

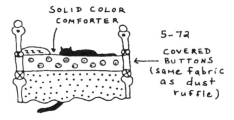

SOLID COLOR COMFORTER

5-72

COVERED BUTTONS (same fabric as dust ruffle)

Knotted Buttons/Frogs

Frogs are especially appropriate for a quilted jacket where their rich ornamentality complements the garment's bulkiness. Frogs also are useful on delicate fabrics (such as lace) on which buttonholes are difficult to make and/or buttoning and unbuttoning causes too much wear and tear.

Materials

1/4" self-filled tubing or corded tubing. For each ball button, you need approximately 10" of self-filled tubing, corded tubing, or store-bought cord/tubing, plus extra for the frog closing(s). The amount of extra cord/tubing you need depends upon the complexity of the frog closing(s). (You also can use other types of cording, such as rounded shoelaces or velvet rope.)

Straight pins

Needle

Thread in the same color as the tubing/cord

Beeswax

Styrofoam board (optional, but helpful)

Fray Check (optional)

How to Do It

1. Make your own self-filled or corded tubing or use a store-bought cord or tubing (Fig. 5-74)

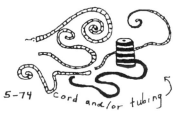

5-74 Cord and/or tubing

2. Pin one end of the tubing/cord to the Styrofoam board (or a sheet of paper). Loop cord as shown (Fig. 5-75). If the tubing/cord has a seam line, keep it on top. This will be the underside of the button.

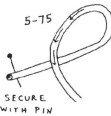

5-75

SECURE WITH PIN IN STYROFOAM

3. Loop again over and under the first loop (Fig. 5-76).

4. Loop a third time, weaving the tubing/cord through the other two loops,

5-76

keeping the loops loose (Fig. 5-77).

5. Ease the loops together, by pulling each end of the tubing/cord (Fig. 5-78).

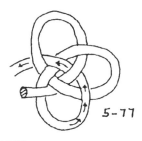

5-77

5-78

PULL HERE

PULL HERE

6. Pull the knot closed, shaping it into a ball and adjusting the loops so they are even (Fig. 5-79).

7. Now trim away excess tubing/cord (to about 1/4" from the knot) and sew the ends to the underside of the button with beeswax-strengthened thread (Fig. 5-80).

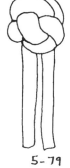

5-79

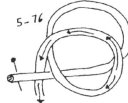

Strengthen with
↓ beeswax

Stitch here

5-80

8. Make the accompanying frog(s) in much the same way as the ball button, except do not pull the loops tightly together into a knot. Instead, keep the knot loose and tack each loop together with beeswax-strengthened thread (Fig. 5-81). Make two frogs (one for each side of the garment) or just one to function as a buttonhole (Fig. 5-82).

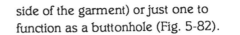

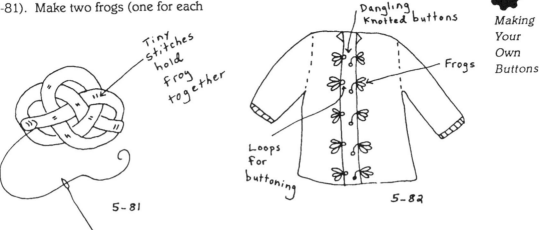

Tiny stitches hold frog together

5-81

Dangling Knotted buttons

Frogs

Loops for buttoning

5-82

Design more elaborate frogs easily by manipulating the tubing/cord into geometric or floral shapes on a Styrofoam board (Fig. 5-83). Or sketch an outline of the frog

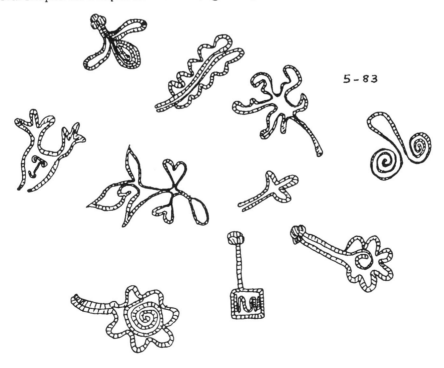

5-83

on cardboard and use it as a pattern. If you need
ideas, look at books on Celtic art or look for a design in
your collection of print fabrics. (Fig. 5-84 shows some
finished frogs.)

*Fig. 5-84 Let your fingers
go wild when designing
frog closures. There's no
rule that they have to look
like these traditional frogs.*

Secure your design with straight pins. If Fray Check
can safely be applied to the tubing/cord you've chosen,
a drop or two will help keep it in place before you
secure the frog permanently with stitches. Otherwise,
use only straight pins to secure the frog as you design it.

Hint: If a larger button is required, refer to knotting/
macrame books for instructions on tying a Monkey's
Fist knot rather than using a thicker tubing/cord to tie
the knot described above. While the Monkey's Fist is a
challenge to learn, it makes a better-looking large
button.

Odd Fact

*Since May 13, 1905, all teddy bears manufac-
tured by Germany's Steiff Company have had a
metal button attached to one ear. Older bears have
silver-colored nickel buttons; modern bears have
brass-colored buttons. A bear with a button that has
an elephant on it is especially rare.*

Leather Buttons

Leather buttons are easy to make at home, and you might already have the necessary materials. For example, soft leather gloves (Fig. 5-85) you no longer wear can be cut into strips and used to make buttons. (Watch Good-

5-85

will and garage sales for candidates.)

For information on covering buttons with leather, see the section on covered buttons.

Leather buttons are appropriate for leather garments and outdoor clothing.

Wrapped Leather Buttons

Materials

Strips of soft leather
Scissors
Needle
Heavy-duty thread in a contrasting color

How to Do It

1. Cut strips of leather approximately 2" to 6" long. The length and width of the strips depend on the thickness of the skin and the size buttons you require (Fig. 5-86).

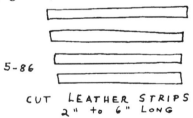

5-86

CUT LEATHER STRIPS
2" to 6" LONG

2. Starting at one end, roll the leather into a tight "log" (Fig. 5-87).

ROLL UP

3. Thread needle and knot thread. Run the thread up through the center of the flap of

leather on top of the roll, hiding the knot. Now secure the leather "log" by wrapping thread around and around the roll. Secure the thread by sewing it around and around this wrapping (Fig. 5-88).

5-88

TIE / WRAP
THEM WITH
COLORED
THREADS

4. Run a new needle and thread into this wrapping to sew buttons to a garment (Fig. 5-89).

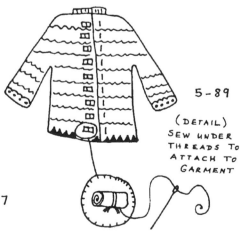

5-89

(DETAIL)
SEW UNDER
THREADS TO
ATTACH TO
GARMENT

LEATHER
LOGS

5-87

Leather Slab Buttons

Materials

Assorted precut leather shapes (available at craft shops or by mail from Tandy Leather Company) (Fig. 5-90)

Leather punch (size 0-6)

Ballpoint pen

Standard-sized eyelets (3/16") and setter kit (optional)

Permanent markers, leather dyes, and/or leather stamps (optional)

CIRCLE
(2 1/4")

LEATHER CONCHA
(2 ")

HEART
(1 3/4")

STAR
(2 ")

LEATHER SLABS for BUTTONS (from TANDY)

5-90

How to Do It

1. Mark hole placement (on what will be the underside of the button) with a ballpoint pen (Fig. 5-91).

MARK HOLES WITH A BALLPOINT PEN 5-91

2. Punch holes with a leather punch (size 0-6) (Fig. 5-92). If you plan to set eyelets in the holes, use a size 6 (3/16") punch.

PUNCH HOLES with A LEATHER PUNCH

5-92

3. If you have an eyelet setting kit, insert and set eyelets in the holes (Fig. 5-93).

SET EYELETS IN HOLES   5-93

4. Decorate buttons with permanent markers, leather stamps, dyes, and/or leather tools (Fig. 5-94).

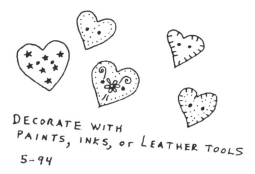

DECORATE WITH PAINTS, INKS, or LEATHER TOOLS

5-94

Metal Buttons

Bottle-Cap Buttons

Friends are often surprised at the
handsome buttons I make out of
ordinary bottle caps. It's worth taking a
trip to the largest liquor store in your
area to peruse the bottle caps. Some of
the beer and mineral water caps are
especially attractive. If you don't like
any of the designs, make buttons
anyway and paint them.

Materials

Acrylic modeling compound (such as
FIMO, Sculpey III or PRO MAT II);
one ounce is enough for ten to twelve
bottle-cap buttons.

Assorted metal bottle caps (Fig. 5-95)

Standard-sized paper clips

Wire cutters

Needle-nosed pliers

Metal skewer or knitting needle

Spatula

Cookie sheet or piece of aluminum foil

Conventional or toaster oven (not
microwave)

Cyanoacrylate (Super Glue) or epoxy

Protective lacquer and/or colored
enamels and paintbrush (optional)

How to Do It

1. Bottle-cap edges often bend when
the caps are removed from bottles.
Therefore, begin by bending the edges

Fig. 5-95 *Bottle caps are surprisingly
attractive for metal buttonmaking.*

back into shape with needle-nosed pliers
(Fig. 5-96). If you don't own needle-
nosed pliers, ordinary pliers will do.

USE PLIERS TO
STRAIGHTEN BENT EDGE

5-96

2. Soften the acrylic modeling compound by following manufacturer's directions (see pages 48–49).

3. Fill the cavity of each bottle cap with acrylic modeling compound (Fig. 5-97). Color choice doesn't matter as this will be the underside of the button.

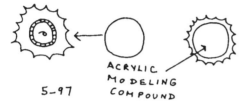

5-97   ACRYLIC MODELING COMPOUND

4. Using wire cutters, cut the rounded tip from a standard-sized paper clip (Fig. 5-98). This U-shaped bit of wire will be the button shank. Imbed one U-shaped wire (prongs down) in the center of each button (Figs. 5-99 and 5-100).

5-98   CUT WITH WIRE CUTTER

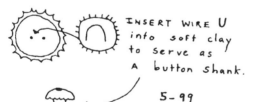

INSERT WIRE U into soft clay to serve as a button shank.

5-99

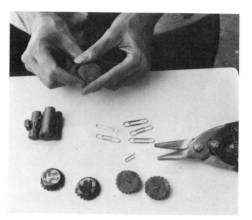

Fig. 5-100 *Insert a U-shaped bit of wire clipped from a paper clip to form the button shank. Photograph by Drew McCalley.*

5. Using a metal skewer or knitting needle, carefully pry the acrylic modeling compound from each bottle cap (Fig. 5-101). Smooth out rough spots with your finger.

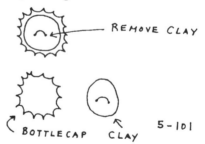

REMOVE CLAY

BOTTLE CAP   CLAY   5-101

6. Leaving the metal shanks in place, bake the buttons on a cookie sheet or piece of aluminum foil (Fig. 5-102) for 15 to 20 minutes at 275-300° F.

5-102

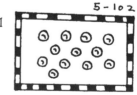

7. Remove buttons from the oven and cool completely.

8. Glue the baked buttons back into their bottle-cap "shells" with cyanoacrylate or epoxy. Also put a drop or two of glue on each side of the button shank (Fig. 5-103).

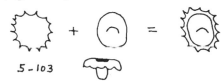

5-103

9. When the glue is dry, coat the back of the buttons with protective lacquer (Fig. 5-104). Use the brand suggested by the manufacturer of your modeling compound. Unlacquered modeling compound can become soiled. In this case, lacquering is optional as the modeling compound will not show.

Paint the button back with clear lacquer.

5-104

10. If you don't like the design on the bottle cap, paint over it with colored enamels. Bottle caps are a nice size for cameolike portraits, or paint them to match a particular fabric (Fig. 5-105).

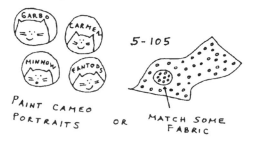

5-105

PAINT CAMEO PORTRAITS   OR   MATCH SOME FABRIC

Coin Buttons

Make buttons from coins left over from a trip to another country. You can even use them on a garment made from fabric purchased on the trip. Also, it's completely legal to make buttons out of U.S. coins; I checked with the U.S. Department of the Treasury.

HOLES   5-106

Materials

Foreign or domestic coins (Fig. 5-106)

Salt, vinegar, and silver polish

Drill and drill bits for drilling metal; the size you use depends on how large you want the holes

Small needle-nosed jeweler's file (optional, but helpful)

Felt-tipped marking pen (fine line)

Vise

How to Do It

1. Clean coins by soaking them overnight in a solution of one teaspoon salt mixed in appoximately 1" of vinegar in a shallow glass dish. Rinse thoroughly (unrinsed coins will be covered with sediment when they dry) and dry completely. Use silver polish to remove any remaining tarnish.

2. Mark hole placement with a felt-tipped pen (Fig. 5-107). Two holes are usually sufficient.

MARK HOLES

5-107

3. Drill holes. Smooth rough edges with the metal file (Fig. 5-108).

SMOOTH
ROUGH
SPOTS

ROUND

FILE 5-108

Plastic Buttons

You can make plastic buttons at home out of acrylic sheet, available at larger hardware stores or plastic suppliers (check the yellow pages under "Plastics"). In addition, some craft stores sell kits for making plastic buttons out of plastic that shrinks when baked. These attractive buttons can be colored with acrylic paints or permanent marking pens.

Materials

Acrylic sheet

Scraps of cardboard

Paper scissors

Grease pencil

Coping saw

Drill and drill bits (the size depends on how large you want the holes)

Plasticine clay

Sandpaper and steel wool

Paints and paintbrushes (optional)

Permanent marking pens (optional)

How to Do It

1. Determine the number and shape of the buttons you require. Make cardboard patterns, place them on the acrylic sheet, and trace around them with a grease pencil. Consider making buttons of different shapes for the same garment. There's no law that says the buttons have to be identical.

2. Cut out the buttons with a coping saw.

3. Sand the buttons. Pay particular attention to the edges, sanding them until they are rounded and smooth.

4. Mark the holes. Before drilling, set the buttons on a piece of plasticine clay to hold them steady. Drill the holes.

5. Acrylic sheet can be decorated with paint or permanent marking pens. If you want to paint your plastic buttons, ask the plastics salesperson for advice. The solvents in some paints damage acrylic sheet.

Dyeing Plastic Buttons

If you have enough plastic buttons and don't want to make more, you might want to dye the ones you have. You can dye some plastic buttons with household dyes.

Materials

Rubber gloves

One package powdered or 1/2-cup liquid dye (light and medium colors work best)

Assortment of light-colored plastic buttons (vinyl buttons take dye best)

Glass, stainless steel, or enamel cooking pot

Wooden stick or spoon for stirring dye

Hot water

Measuring cup

Heavy-duty thread

How to Do It

1. Put on rubber gloves and then dissolve one package of powdered dye in one pint of very hot (140° F) water. Or mix 1/2-cup liquid dye and one quart of very hot water (140° F). Don't use boiling water or the buttons might melt (Fig. 5-109).

2. Thread one button onto a length of heavy-duty thread and dunk it in the dye solution. Swish it around, pulling it out from time to time to check the color.

3. When you achieve a color you like, remove the button from the dye solution and rinse well in warm running water (Fig. 5-110).

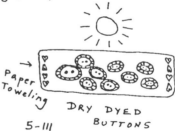

4. Lay button on paper toweling to dry (Fig. 5-111).

5. If you like the results, thread more buttons on the string and dye them in the same manner (Fig. 5-112).

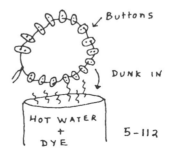

Shell Buttons

If you live near a river, you can try your hand at making buttons from freshwater clam shells. The rest of us can use the shells collected on our last vacation to the seashore. If you're like me, that collection is stuffed in a drawer. Now you'll be glad you saved them because the sturdier shells can be made into buttons.

Materials

Assorted shells (at least 1/8" thick)

Drill and drill bits (the size depends on how large you want the holes)

Plasticine clay

Enamel or glass cooking pot

Bleach

Water

Mineral oil or protective lacquer

How to Do It

1. If the shells are dirty, soak them overnight in a weak solution of bleach and water (Fig. 5-113). This should remove dirt and other evidence of life in the sea.

5-113

Bleach and water solution

2. Examine the shell to determine where to drill the holes. Two considerations should influence your decision: the shell's shape and the strength of the wall of the shell at the location of each hole. Position the holes so the shell will hang well when sewn to a garment. You don't want it to be top heavy. Plan to drill the holes at thick places on the shell so that they are strong enough to withstand repeated buttoning. Mark the hole placement with a pencil.

3. Place each shell on a piece of plasticine clay to hold it in place and then drill the holes (Fig. 5-114).

5-114

Lump of Plasticine to hold shell steady for drilling

4. If you like color, shells can be dyed with some success. Early manufacturers had difficulty obtaining uniform colors. However, modern aniline dyes work beautifully.

If you have little experience with dyeing, try dyeing shells with all-purpose household dye. A flyer entitled "Tinting Small Vinyl Plastic Items" (available from Rit Consumer Service, P.O. Box 21070, Indianapolis, IN 46221; send a #10 stamped, self-addressed envelope) is helpful. The instructions also apply to shells. Rit consumer experts advise using light to medium colors rather than dark ones. Dark colors tend to produce "off" shades.

Ordinary food coloring can also be used with some success. It produces subtle shades but is not colorfast. For those considering dyeing mother-of-pearl buttons from their button box: Food coloring will not "take" well on smooth, glossy surfaces. It works better on surfaces with a porous, opaque appearance.

5. Rub dyed shell buttons with mineral oil or spray or brush them with protective lacquer. Shell buttons dyed with food coloring should be coated with clear acrylic or colorless nail polish to preserve the color.

Wooden Buttons

Select a wood that complements the fabric on which you plan to sew the buttons. Smooth, highly polished buttons made from hardwood look terrific on a classic navy blazer (Fig. 5-115). Driftwood twigs, on the other hand, make fun buttons for a rugged sweater (Fig. 5-116).

Wooden moldings from a lumberyard, sawed into button-sized sections and spray-painted gold, make elegant buttons for a party dress (Fig. 5-117).

CLASSIC BLAZER

VTG

Polished Hardwood Buttons

5-115

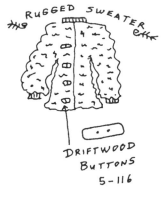

RUGGED SWEATER

DRIFTWOOD BUTTONS
5-116

★ PARTY DRESS ★

Fancy Wooden Molding cut into sections + sprayed gold

5-117

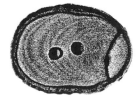

Materials

Wood of your choice (hardwood, drift-wood, wooden molding, etc.)

Pencil

Scraps of cardboard

Paper scissors

Coping saw

Drill and drill bits (the size depends on how large you want the holes)

Sandpaper and/or steel wool

Plasticine clay

Clear protective lacquer, metallic paints, colorless shoe polish, or furniture polish or wax

Paintbrush (optional)

How to Do It

1. Determine the number and shape of the buttons you require. Make a cardboard pattern and use it to draw your design(s) on the wood. Consider making buttons of different shapes for the same garment. There's no law that says the buttons have to be identical (Fig. 5-118).

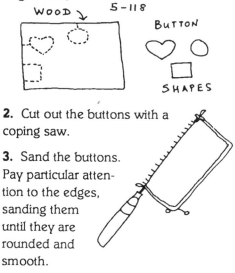

2. Cut out the buttons with a coping saw.

3. Sand the buttons. Pay particular attention to the edges, sanding them until they are rounded and smooth.

4. You can leave the buttons plain, coat them with protective finishes, paint or dye them, use a paper-backed fusible web (such as Pellon's Wonder-Under) to bond fabric to the wood, or stencil them. Here's how:

Protective Finishes

Coat the buttons with clear lacquer or paint. If you are uncertain about what kind of lacquer to use, refer to any general purpose woodworking book for advice. Two common household substances can be used to finish wooden buttons—colorless shoe polish and furniture polish/wax. These finishes are not as durable as lacquer (Fig. 5-119).

Mark holes. Before drilling, set the buttons on a piece of plasticine clay to hold them steady (Fig. 5-120). Drill the holes.

Dye

Additional materials: Liquid household dye (Rit or Tintex), clean rags, and rubber gloves.

If you want colorful wooden buttons, consider staining them with liquid household dye. Pine, oak, and cherry all absorb dye beautifully; bamboo does not dye well. Experiment on a scrap of wood first to learn how to achieve the color you desire. The amount of dye you need depends on the intensity of the color you want to achieve. A quarter of a bottle is sufficient for approximately twenty buttons. If you don't want your hands to match your buttons, wear rubber gloves.

Use the dye directly from the bottle, or, to achieve a more subtle color, dilute the dye with hot water. Spread the dye evenly with a brush, soft cloth, or sponge until the wood is well saturated

(Fig. 5-121). Let the buttons dry for five minutes. Then wipe off the excess dye with a lint-free cloth. Repeat these steps until the wood is the desired color. Soft woods are more absorbent and require fewer coats (one or two) than hard woods (up to six). Let the buttons dry thoroughly. Then rub them with steel wool and polish them with a soft cloth.

Finish buttons with protective lacquer, colorless shoe polish, or furniture polish/wax.

Mark the holes. Before drilling, set the buttons on a piece of plasticine clay to hold them steady. Drill the holes.

Bonded Fabric

See Fig. 5-122.

Additional materials: paper-backed

fusible web (such as Pellon's Wonder-Under), fabric, sewing scissors, press cloth and steam iron, enamel and/or fabric paints (optional).

If you use Wonder-Under to fuse fabric to wooden buttons, place a piece of Wonder-Under, rough side down, on

the wrong side of the fabric. Press for three seconds with a hot, dry iron (Fig. 5-123). Let cool.

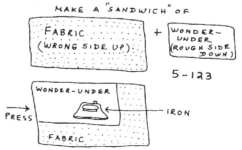

Set wooden button shapes on this fabric and trace around them with a pencil. Cut out the fabric shapes (Fig. 5-124).

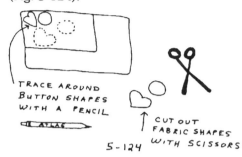

TRACE AROUND BUTTON SHAPES WITH A PENCIL

CUT OUT FABRIC SHAPES WITH SCISSORS

5-124

Fuse buttons one at a time following these steps: Set iron at "wool" steam setting. Peel off paper backing, position fabric (coated side down) on the wooden shape, and cover with a damp press cloth. Press for ten seconds (Fig. 5-125).

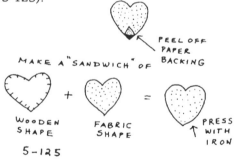

PEEL OFF PAPER BACKING

MAKE A "SANDWICH" OF

WOODEN SHAPE + FABRIC SHAPE = PRESS WITH IRON

5-125

Add an extra touch by painting around the edges of the buttons with a solid line of enamel, or embellish the fabric with fabric paint (Fig. 5-126).

FABRIC PAINT

PAINT EDGE WITH ENAMEL

ENAMEL PAINT

5-126

Spray or paint the buttons with clear lacquer so that they'll survive laundering.

Mark the holes. Before drilling, set the buttons on a piece of plasticine clay to hold them steady. Drill the holes.

Stencil

Additional materials: precut stencils (or stiff paper/plastic and scissors), stenciling brush, and acrylic paints.

Since wooden buttons take paint well, stenciling is also a possibility. Stenciling requires few materials and is excellent for achieving a "country" look (Fig. 5-127).

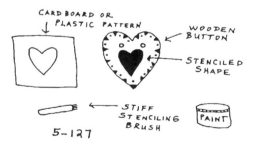

CARDBOARD OR PLASTIC PATTERN

WOODEN BUTTON

STENCILED SHAPE

STIFF STENCILING BRUSH

PAINT

5-127

Use precut stencil forms, or cut your own out of stiff paper or plastic. Lay the stencil form over the button and apply acrylic paint with a stiff stenciling brush. Don't overload the brush; a little paint works best.

Let buttons dry before coating them with protective lacquer.

Mark the holes. Before drilling, set the buttons on a piece of plasticine clay to hold them steady. Drill the holes.

Buttons from Odds and Ends

Fig. 5-128 Scrabble tiles, anagrams, checkers, and children's wooden toys make whimsical buttons. Fantods the cat wouldn't make a very good button, however; he's too big.

Some of the most imaginative buttons didn't start out as buttons. They had other lives as other things. You can make a button out of most any small item, provided you know how to drill holes. The possibilities are limited only by your imagination.

For example, remember the Scrabble game that your son "destroyed" by gluing many of the letters to his science project? Don't throw it out. Make buttons from the remaining tiles, perhaps for that shirt you've been promising to make for him.

Your daughter might not play with the wooden barn and tiny farm animals anymore, but she'd probably love a sweater with animal buttons. You'd better ask her before drilling holes in the cow, however.

Materials

Miscellaneous button-sized household objects such as spare wooden game pieces (anagram or Scrabble tiles, bingo numbers and markers, checkers, dominos, dice, mah-jongg tiles), small toys, wooden thread spools, etc. (See Fig. 5-128 on the previous page.)

Drill and drill bits (the size depends on how large you want the holes)

Vise (optional)

Coping saw (in case you want to alter the shape of an object)

Sandpaper

Plasticine clay

Pencil

How to Do It

1. With a pencil, mark the hole placement on the items you plan to drill. You'll need to decide how many holes to make on each object. Heavier items (such as small toys) require four holes;

smaller objects only require two (Fig. 5-129).

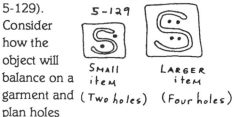

Consider how the object will balance on a garment and plan holes accordingly. Some objects are heavier at one end than at the other, so you'll need to allow for that.

2. Place the potential button on a piece of plasticine clay or clamp it in a vise to hold it steady during drilling (Fig. 5-130). Drill the holes.

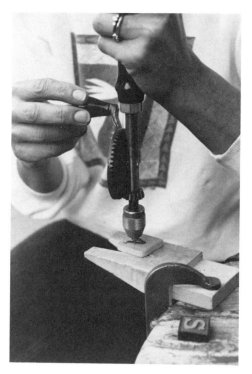

Fig. 5-130 *Drill two holes and you're ready to sew the button to a garment.*

1 2 3 Additional Ideas 1 2 3

*Making
Your
Own
Buttons*

Spell out the word "BUTTONS" in Scrabble or anagram tiles and sew the seven buttons on a dress or jacket (Fig. 5-131). You can do the

5-131

same with personal names (Fig. 5-132).

5-132

Spell out your pet's name in the same way. The buttons are fun sewn onto a cat or dog collar (Fig. 5-133).

5-133

Spell out the word "CAT" or "DOG" in Scrabble or anagram tiles

and combine those buttons with appropriate animal-shaped buttons (Fig. 5-134).

5-134

If you live near a large city, visit Chinatown for wooden game sets. The game pieces are often embellished with animals and Chinese characters. They make wonderful buttons for quilted jackets and children's clothing (Fig. 5-135).

5-135

Split an old wooden thread spool in half to make two buttons. You can cut it so the top and bottom labels show, or lengthwise (Fig. 5-136). Consider dyeing the spools with household dye (see page 79).

SPOOL BUTTONS

OR

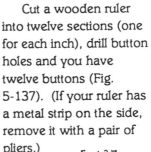

5-136

Cut a wooden ruler into twelve sections (one for each inch), drill button holes and you have twelve buttons (Fig. 5-137). (If your ruler has a metal strip on the side, remove it with a pair of pliers.)

5-137

1 2 3 4 5 6 7 8 9 10 11 12
♥ MY LITTLE RULER ♥

RULER BUTTONS

Remember that the possibilities are limited only by your imagination. If you make buttons out of something unusual, I'd love to hear about them. Please write to me either care of Poor Little Isabel's (address in Mail-Order Sources for Buttons in the Appendices) or care of my publisher.

6. Creating Button Jewelry

While most buttons serve a functional purpose, others are there to enhance a design or provoke a smile. In some cultures buttons are worn in addition to jewelry to show off the wealth of the wearer.

In fact, buttons have been used as mere ornamentation for centuries. Accounts from the time assert that France's Francis I (1494–1547) wore a black velvet suit embellished with 13,600 gold buttons to a conference with England's King Henry VIII (1491–1547). We can only imagine Henry's reaction, but it was probably jealousy. Henry had his own collection of fancy buttons.

With all this extravagance, even the rich must have felt the need to economize (or at least to fool others); the first costume jewelry was made in France during the reign of Louis XIV (1638–1715).

Journals and letters of eighteenth- and nineteenth-century travelers to Russia describe the opulence of the Russian nobility, who reportedly spent much of their money on clothes and jewelry. Even men wore diamond buttons.

Jewelry was also important to Russian peasants, who handed it down from generation to generation. While some jewelry was worn for luck or to ward off evil, most was worn to show the wearer's wealth. Buttons obtained from traders were valuable to some people and sometimes were used to decorate clothing lavishly.

According to historian Charles Holme, "A Swedish peasant-bride in olden times resembled a jeweller's shop window, so covered was she with silver ornaments from head to toe."[7] These ornaments included many silver buttons. On the island of Öland, custom demanded that the silver-encumbered bride run on foot from her house to the church. Holme cites an account (circa 1760) that describes this ritual:

"The running is troublesome enough, for she wears a silver crown on her head, weighing two to three pounds, besides having several kirtles on and a number of jewels consisting of glass or bits of broken mirror set in pewter or lead.

"A number of bridesmaids fell behind in the race, and so the bride had time to recover breath in the church porch before these attendants were all assembled again."

Making Your Own Button Jewelry

Maybe you don't want to resemble a Swedish peasant bride, but you can make wonderful jewelry with buttons. A few prized buttons combined with other materials can add up to something personal and just as precious as the bride's embellishments.

Most of the materials I use in this chapter are easy to find (plate 16). Here's some information to help you locate them.

Jewelry findings, such as **pin backs, earring backs, necklace clasps,** and **stickpins**, are available at some craft stores, at jewelers' supply stores, and by mail. Consult Other Button Resources in the Appendices for a list of mail-order sources.

Monofilament fishing line is available at hardware stores and tackle shops.

Needle-nosed pliers have pointed "noses." They're available at hardware stores, at jewelers' supply stores, and by mail. Consult Other Button Resources in the Appendices for a list of mail-order sources.

Wire clippers are available at hardware stores and jewelers' supply stores.

 # Button Medallions

French Medallion

These medallions were inspired by some on the skirt of a nineteenth-century young woman's festival costume from the Tula Province of the U.S.S.R. They make a sentimental, "something old/something blue" gift for a bride-to-be. Use a button from the family button box and blue ribbon to make a medallion for her garter or a rosette for her hair. Some of the rosettes on the Russian skirt were also embellished with long ribbons (Fig. 6-1).

6-1

Rosettes with Buttons

Some with long ribbons

Young woman's festival dress; Tula Province U.S.S.R - Mid-19th century

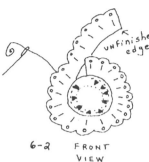

*The
Button
Lover's
Book*

6-2   FRONT
        VIEW

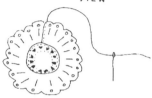

FRONT VIEW   6-3

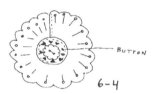

6-4

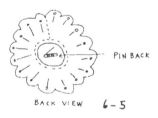

BACK VIEW   6-5

Fig. 6-6 *Button medallions
are the perfect solution for
the "something old, some-
thing new, something
borrowed, something blue"
wedding tradition.*

Materials

A favorite button (antique metal or mother-of-pearl)

Straight pins

Thread and needle

Pin back (optional)

Enough lace, ribbon, or ruffling to form into a circle under the button

Felt circle or embroidered patch (about twice as big as the button)

How to Do It

1. Ease the lace, ribbon, or ruffling into a circle by gathering it on one edge and pinning or basting the material approximately 1/4" from the edges of the underside of the felt circle or embroidered patch (Fig. 6-2).

2. Sew the ruffle securely to the felt circle or embroidered patch (Fig. 6-3).

3. Sew the button in the center front of the felt circle or embroidered patch (Fig. 6-4).

4. Sew a pin back to the back of the ruffled circle or sew the circle to a bride's elastic garter (found in most bridal salons) or to a garment (Fig. 6-5). (Fig. 6-6 shows finished medallions. Also see plates 13A and 13B.)

Plates 9A and B *Children's clothing designers at After the Stork combined different colored buttons and fabrics to create a fun pair of overalls. Photographs courtesy of and copyright by After the Stork. (Address: 1501 12th St., Albuquerque, New Mexico 87104)*

Plate 10 *Patrick Kelly-inspired jacket from Burda (pattern number: 5295B). Photograph courtesy of Verlag Aenne Burda/Pattern Division.*

Plate 11A *(above) I photographed this vest at the craft fair. The seamstress cleverly covered the buttons with embroidered Chinese fabric.*

Plate 11B *(right) Buttons of several colors add pep to this simple black dress. No law says that the buttons all have to be the same. Photograph courtesy of Verlag Aenne Burda/Pattern Division (pattern number: 5159).*

Plate 12 *Small pins require few materials so they're great projects to carry to the beach or the doctor's office. Stuff the pins with polyester fiberfill and decorate them liberally with buttons. Photograph courtesy of Simplicity Pattern Company, Inc. (pattern number: 9688, June 1990).*

Button and Bead Medallion

Fig. 6-7 *Make a button pendant to wear with your "opening night" dress. These each took me one afternoon.*

A medallion cut from an old silk tie forms the center-piece for this pendant or small evening purse. Even the ugliest tie has possibilities. Surround or partially cover the medallion with buttons and you've truly made a "silk purse from a sow's ear" (Fig. 6-7).

Materials

Men's silk tie	Scissors
Felt	Needle
Assorted buttons and beads	Thread
	Polyester fiberfill (if
Cord	making a pendant)

How to Do It

1. Cut a medallion from the silk tie. Ties with pictures printed on them are appropriate and fun. For example, I used a tie with reindeer printed on it and cut around the picture. The resulting silk medallion is approximately 2" by 2-1/2". Your medallion could be larger or smaller, depending on your taste in necklaces.

Next, cut two pieces of felt in the same shape, one or two inches larger in all directions than the silk medallion (Fig. 6-8).

2. By hand or machine, appliqué the silk medallion in the center of one of the felt pieces (Fig. 6-9).

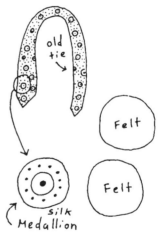

6-8

appliqué silk medallion to felt circle

6-9

3. Embellish the piece with buttons and/or beads, leaving 1/4" at the edges for a seam allowance (Fig. 6-10).

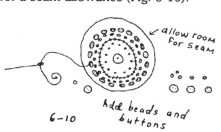

6-10

4. With right sides together, sew the two pieces of felt together 1/4" from the edge, as though you were making a pillow. Leave an open space to enable you to turn the seams to the inside (Fig. 6-11).

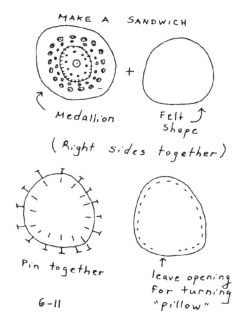

6-11

5. Turn the seams to the inside (Fig. 6-12). If making a pendant, stuff the pillow with polyester fiberfill

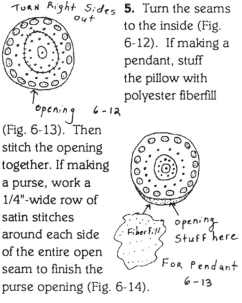

(Fig. 6-13). Then stitch the opening together. If making a purse, work a 1/4"-wide row of satin stitches around each side of the entire open seam to finish the purse opening (Fig. 6-14).

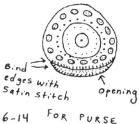

6. Attach a cord to form either a necklace or purse handle (Fig. 6-15).

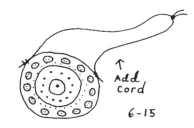

(Fig. 6-7 on the previous page shows finished pendants.)

🌀 Button Earrings 🌀

Button earrings are simple to make and are a perfect use for a special pair of matching antique buttons. Jewelry findings are available at jewelers' supply stores, at craft shops, or by mail. Consult Other Button Resources in the Appendices for mail-order sources.

Materials

Two buttons

Wire clippers (if the buttons have metal shanks)

Metal file (if the buttons have metal shanks)

Pierced or clip earring findings

Cyanoacrylate (Super Glue)

Acrylic modeling compound (optional)

How to Do It

1. If the buttons have shanks, remove the wire with wire clippers and smooth remaining points of metal from the back of the button with a metal file (Fig. 6-16).

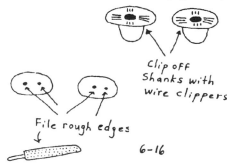

Clip off Shanks with wire clippers

File rough edges

6-16

2. If the buttons have holes, you can leave them open or make plugs out of acrylic modeling compound. Bake the plugs (according to the directions that came with the modeling compound). After the plugs have cooled, glue them into the holes with cyanoacrylate (Fig. 6-17). If you don't want to make plugs but still want to hide the holes, glue beads or smaller buttons over them (Fig. 6-18).

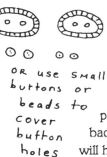

(Acrylic Modeling compound plugs for button holes   6-17

OR use small buttons or beads to cover button holes

6-18

3. For pierced earrings, position a finding toward the top back of each earring. For clip-on earrings, position the earring back so the earrings will hang properly on your ear. Examine other earrings in your collection to assist in this decision (Fig. 6-19).

4. Glue the findings to the buttons with cyanoacrylate. Let the glue dry completely before wearing the earrings.

Post finding   OR   Back of button

clip-on finding   6-19

Button Cuff Bracelet

Fig. 6-20 I used metal buttons with words on them for my button cuff bracelets. They're easy to make. Photograph by Drew McCalley.

This sturdy bangle bracelet has plastic canvas core and is perfect for showcasing a collection of special buttons. For example, I used a selection of flat metal buttons embossed with product names and textures (Fig. 6-20).

Bay Area artist Kathy Cargile makes similar bracelets by sewing buttons to wide strips of elastic.

Materials

Plastic canvas

Paper and fabric scissors

Plastic tape

Quilt batting

Felt

Assorted buttons and beads

Thread

Needle

Embroidery floss

How to Do It

1. Cut a length of plastic canvas to serve as the core of the bracelet. Form it into a bracelet shape and secure the ends with tape (Fig. 6-21). You should be able to slip the plastic canvas bracelet on and off easily, but don't make it too loose. My bracelet is 1-1/2" x 10".

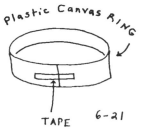

2. Cut a length of quilt batting with the same dimensions as the length of plastic canvas. Secure the quilt batting around the plastic canvas bracelet with basting stitches or tape (Fig. 6-22).

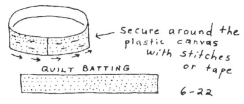

3. Cut a piece of felt with which to cover the plastic canvas bracelet. The felt should be the same length and a bit more than twice as wide as the bracelet. Wrap the felt around the plastic canvas core and secure it with pins or basting stitches (Fig. 6-23).

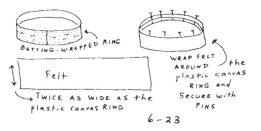

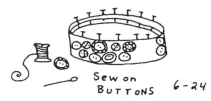

Creating Button Jewelry

4. Sew the buttons to the bracelet with heavy-duty thread (Fig. 6-24). Don't be afraid to stack the buttons over each other. Don't be too concerned with the neatness of the stitches on the inside of the bracelet. You'll eventually cover them with another piece of felt.

5. Add beads or embellish with embroidery (optional) (Fig. 6-25).

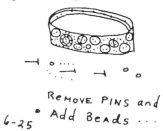

6. Cut another piece of felt the same width and length as the core of plastic canvas and sew it to the inside of the bracelet to conceal your stitching (Fig. 6-26).

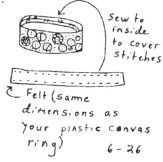

(Fig. 6-20 on the previous page shows finished bracelets.)

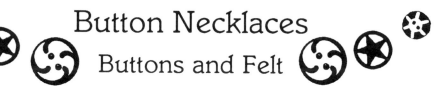

Button Necklaces
Buttons and Felt

This necklace was inspired by an ethnic piece from Nepal made with brass beads and red fabric disks.

Materials

50-100 buttons of uniform size (plain metal buttons are wonderful with the colored felt)

20-30 small beads

Monofilament fishing line, dental floss, or heavy-duty thread

Needle

Scraps of colored felt

Scissors

Clasp finding

Wooden Scrabble tray (optional, but helpful)

How to Do It

1. Stand in front of a mirror and hold the heavy-duty thread, monofilament fishing line, or dental floss around your neck to determine how long to make the necklace (Fig. 6-27). Or measure a favorite necklace and cut that amount of thread. If using heavy-duty thread, use a double strand.

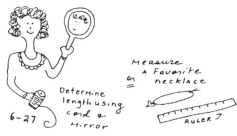

2. Thread the needle with the thread and knot the end.

3. Cut a variety of small squares or circles of colored felt. Make the pieces a bit smaller than the buttons you've chosen.

You'll need at least three pieces of felt for every button you use (Fig. 6-28).

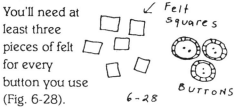

4. Thread on half of the beads. When you wear the necklace, these beads will rest on the back of your neck, enabling the necklace to lie flat (Fig. 6-29).

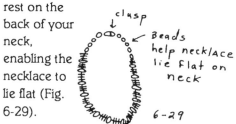

5. Before threading on the buttons and bits of felt, experiment with the necklace design by arranging the buttons and felt in rows. I arrange the buttons and felt on one of the wooden trays from our Scrabble game (Fig. 6-30). Try different arrangements until you find one you like. Use at least three pieces of felt between each button or group of buttons.

6. Thread on the buttons and felt pieces (Fig. 6-31).

7. Thread on the remaining beads (Fig. 6-32).

8. Attach the clasp finding (Fig. 6-33).

(Fig. 6-34 shows finished necklaces; plate 14A shows a creative variation.)

Fig. 6-34 *Button 'n' felt necklaces adorn an antique doll.*

Mother-of-Pearl String

Here's something elegant to make with your treasured mother-of-pearl buttons. Why let them sit in the button box? If you later need one, simply shorten the necklace.

Materials

Large sew-through mother-of-pearl buttons (all the same size)

Needle

Monofilament fishing line, dental floss, or heavy-duty thread

Scissors

Clasp finding

How to Do It

1. Thread needle and knot thread.

2. Sew **up** through the left hole of a button and **down** through the right hole (Fig. 6-35).

6-35

3. Pick up another button and sew **down** through the left hole and **up** through the right (Fig. 6-36).

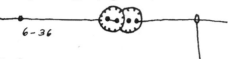

4. Continue attaching buttons in this manner until the necklace is the length you want (Fig. 6-37).

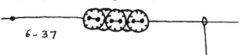

5. Attach a clasp finding (Fig. 6-38).

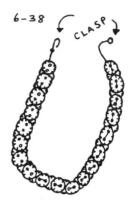

 # Button Pins

Materials

Favorite large two- or four-hole button (Bakelite and celluloid buttons from the 1920s work well) or stack buttons of descending sizes on top of one another

Heavy-duty thread of the same color (or a contrasting color)

Pin back

Cyanoacrylate (Super Glue) or epoxy

Needle

How to Do It

1. Using a double, unknotted thread, sew through two of the holes so both ends of the thread are on the back of the button (Fig. 6-39).

2. Apply a dab of cyanoacrylate or epoxy to the back of the pin back (Fig. 6-40).

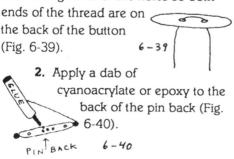

3. Now sew both ends of the thread through the holes in the back of the pin back, so it rests on the back of the button (Fig. 6-41).

4. Tie the threads together and knot securely to attach the pin back to the button (Fig. 6-42).

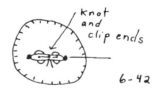

5. Let glue dry thoroughly before wearing the pin. (Plate 14B shows an elaborate variation.)

✸ Button Stickpins ✸

Make a button stickpin for a blazer lapel or hat. The project takes about five minutes.

Materials

Favorite button (shank-type works best)
Stickpin finding
Needle
Heavy-duty thread

How to Do It

1. Remove the protective tip from the stickpin (Fig. 6-43).

2. Insert the stickpin through the button shank until it reaches the top (Fig. 6-44).

3. Sew the button securely in place at the top of the stickpin (Fig. 6-45).

4. Replace the protective tip.

Additional Ideas for Button Jewelry

Make rings with buttons by pushing flexible wire through two of the holes (or through the shank) and bending the wire to form a ring that fits your finger (Fig. 6-46). Secure the wire

by twisting it around the shank several times or around itself (Fig. 6-47). You can make especially attractive rings with antique metal buttons and copper or brass wire

from the hardware store. Rings made with large metal buttons make great stage jewelry because they look terribly expensive from the tenth row. (Be careful: Copper and brass wire turns some people's skin green.)

Use needle-nosed pliers and a hammer to make "add-on" jewelry with buttons, beads and

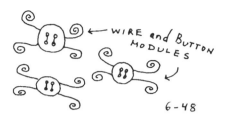

← WIRE and BUTTON MODULES

6-48

wire (Fig. 6-48). String several of these modules together to make a bracelet or necklace (Fig. 6-49).

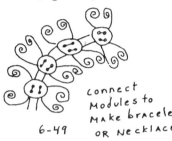

connect Modules to MAke bracelet OR NecklAce

6-49

Cover a fabric watchband with buttons (Fig. 6-50).

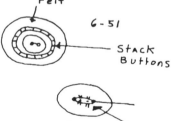

6-50

Sew a stack of buttons to a circle of felt and attach a pin or earring back (Fig. 6-51).

Felt

6-51

Stack Buttons

BACK VIEW

PIN BACK

Crochet a bracelet with elastic gimp, using a size 6–9 crochet hook. Select an elastic that will blend in with the buttons you've chosen. For example, use white elastic with white buttons; black elastic

with black buttons, etc. The elastic shouldn't be obvious.

Chain fifty to sixty stitches to form a length that fits snugly but comfortably around your wrist. (If you don't know how to crochet, consult any crochet manual for instructions. It's easy.) Make the length wider by adding three rows of double crochet. Knot the elastic and hide the end by weaving it into the bracelet.

Use a large-eyed needle to attach buttons to the mesh with more elastic gimp/cord (Fig. 6-52).

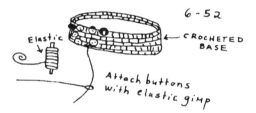

6-52

Elastic

CROCHETED BASE

Attach buttons with elastic gimp

Weave rows of seed beads among the buttons (optional), or add plastic toys or animals (Fig. 6-53). Pierce holes

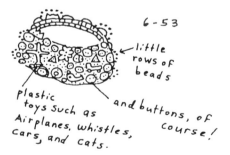

6-53

little rows of beads

and buttons, of course!

Plastic toys such as Airplanes, whistles, cars, and cats.

in the toys with a hot needle. Be sure to hold the needle with a pot holder so you won't burn yourself.

Cuff buttons and cuff links were first worn in the seventeenth century. If you have four matching shank-type buttons and want to use them for something special, make cuff links. Connect pairs of buttons with wire or cord. The connecting length often varies, so measure a favorite cuff link to determine the amount of cord or wire you require. Then string each pair of buttons on a separate but equal length of wire or cord (Fig. 6-54).

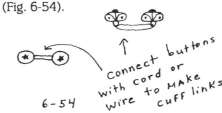

Sew buttons to a ribbon and wear it as a necklace (Fig. 6-55).

Odd Fact

The popular song "Buttons and Bows" was written by Jay Livingston and Ray Evans in 1948. The tune was introduced by Bob Hope and Jane Russell in the movie The Paleface *(1948). "Buttons and Bows" won the Academy Award for best song. The version of the song recorded by Dinah Shore for Columbia sold over a million records.*

 # 7. Button Toys

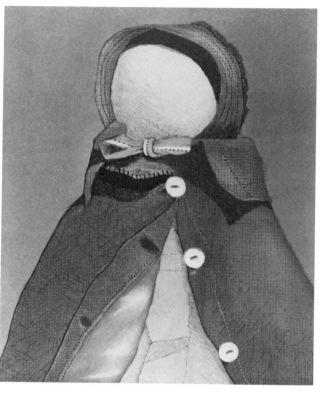

Fig. 7-1 *"Amish Doll," by Gordon Cook. Photograph courtesy of Liadain O'Donoven-Cook.*

If your child is too young to play with the family button box, consider using selected buttons to make toys. Be very careful, however; close supervision is still a must. The U.S. Consumer Safety Commission warns that children under three should not be allowed to play with small objects that they might swallow.

Amish dolls (Fig. 7-1) are wonderful for a very young child because they traditionally have no facial features (that is, no button eyes). If you put buttons on the doll's clothes, save them for when the child is older.

✹ Button Abacus ✹

The first calculator, the abacus, was probably made in Babylonia. The instrument was refined and used by the Chinese and other Asians, Arabs, and Romans. An early Chinese abacus (sixth century B.C.) consisted of stonelike beads strung on a wooden frame with wire (Fig. 7-2). The traditional abacus has nine rows, each with ten beads. These rows represent units of ascending value (reading from right to left): units, tens, hundreds, thousands, etc.

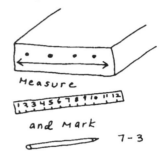

7-2

Be ready for the next time the batteries fail in your pocket calculator. Make an abacus out of buttons. Our button abacus has four rows and is appropriate for simple calculations and for teaching addition and subtraction.

Materials

Cardboard shirt or dress box (at least 2" deep)

Heavy-duty thread

Needle

Ruler

Pencil

Metal skewer or knitting needle

Assorted two-hole buttons (12 red, 12 blue, 12 yellow, and 12 green)

How to Make It

1. With the ruler, divide each end of the box into five sections. Mark each section 1/2" down from the edge of the box with a pencil. When you're finished measuring, you will have four pencil marks along each end (Fig. 7-3).

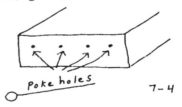

Measure

and Mark

7-3

2. Use the metal skewer or knitting needle to punch a hole at each pencil mark (Fig. 7-4).

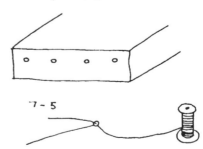

Poke holes

7-4

3. Thread the needle with heavy-duty thread, but don't break off the thread from the spool (Fig. 7-5).

7-5

4. Now hold a red button against the **outside** of the box directly over the first punched hole (Fig. 7-6). Push the

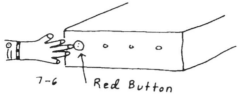

7-6 | Red Button

needle through one of the holes in the button and through the first punched hole (Fig. 7-7).

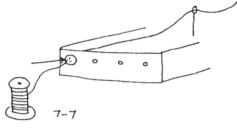

7-7

5. Pull the thread through the side of the box. Now thread ten red buttons onto the thread (Fig. 7-8).

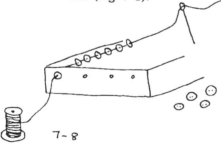

7-8

6. Hold another red button against the **outside** of the box directly over the punched hole at the other end of the

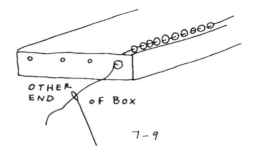

OTHER END of Box

7-9

box (Fig. 7-9) (the end that doesn't have a red button on the outside). Push the needle from the **inside** of the box through the punched hole and through one of the holes in the button. Now push the needle through the other hole on that button and back through the same punched hole (Fig. 7-10).

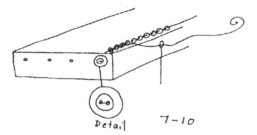

Detail 7-10

7. Return the thread through the remaining hole in each of the red buttons you suspended across the box, through the first punched hole, and through the remaining hole in the red button placed outside of the box (Fig. 7-11). Snip the

7-11

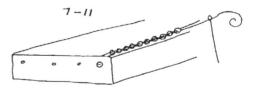

threads, leaving enough to tie the thread ends to secure that row of buttons. Tie a secure knot, pulling the thread taut, so that the string of buttons doesn't sag against the floor of the box (Fig. 7-12).

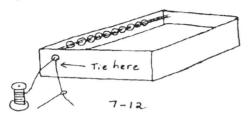

8. Repeat the last five steps with the blue, yellow, and green buttons. When you finish, you will have four lines of buttons across the inside of the box (Fig. 7-13).

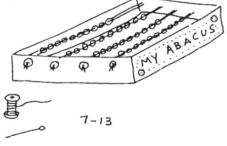

How to Use It

1. Reading from the right, the first row of buttons represents single units of one through ten. The second row represents tens. The third row represents hundreds. The fourth row represents thousands. Calculations are performed by moving buttons from one side of the abacus to the other.

2. For addition, start with all buttons on one side of the abacus. To add the number twelve to the number twenty-three, move two buttons in the first row to the other side of the abacus. Then move one button in the second row to the other side of the abacus. These buttons represent the number twelve. Now move three more buttons in the first row to join the first two buttons you moved. Next move two more buttons in the second row. These buttons represent the number twenty-three. You should now have five buttons in the first group and three buttons in the second. These buttons represent the number thirty-five—the sum of twelve plus twenty-three. Now you try it.

3. For subtraction, start with all buttons on one side of the abacus. To subtract twelve from twenty-three, move three buttons in the first row to the other side of the abacus. Then move two buttons in the second row to the other side of the abacus. Now move two buttons from the first row and one button from the second row back. One button remains in the first row and one in the second. These buttons represent the number eleven, which is the correct answer. Now you try it.

Button Dancer

It's possible to transform a handful of buttons and beads into a special gift in about 15 minutes. Make a button dancer (Fig. 7-14). She makes a great baby gift or (made with heavy string) a whimsical bob for a key chain. If you make her for a baby, be sure to include a note to the mom: "Hang the button dancer well out of Kaitlin's reach."

Materials

Two- and/or four-hole buttons of various sizes and colors

Large-eyed needle

Heavy-duty thread or string

Assorted beads

Enamels or permanent markers

Fray Check

Fig. 7-14 *I tied a small toy to the hand of one of my button dancers. I'm thinking of making more to attach to a Christmas wreath.*

How to Make It

1. Decide on a color scheme. Then select a large bead for the dancer's head, a smaller bead for her neck, an assortment of like-sized buttons for her body and hat (fifteen to twenty buttons), four smaller buttons for hands and feet, and an assortment of small beads for her legs and arms (Fig. 7-15). Lay your design out on a table before stringing to get an idea of how the dancer will look.

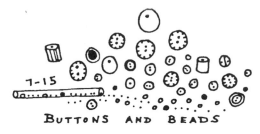

7-15

BUTTONS AND BEADS

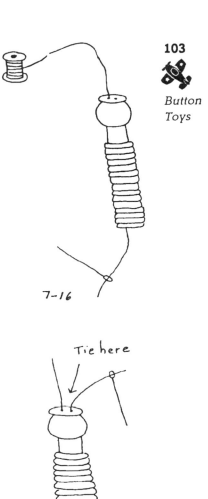

7-16

Tie here

7-17

2. Thread a length of heavy-duty thread (approximately 1-1/2' long). Don't knot the thread. Now string on the hat button, head button, neck button, and body buttons (Fig. 7-16).

3. Double the thread back through another hole in each of the body buttons and back through the neck and head. Now go through another hole in the hat button and tie the ends of the thread together to secure the top of the dancer's body (Fig. 7-17). This thread can serve as a hanger or you can snip off the ends after tying.

4. Cut two lengths (each approximately 10" to 12") of thread for the dancer's arms.

5. Lay one length of thread on the table. Now lay the dancer on her back on top of the thread so that the

7-18

7-19

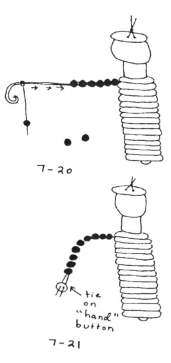

7-20

7-21

tie
on
"hand"
button

thread rests just under the button under the neck bead (Fig. 7-18). Pick up the right end of the thread and drape it over to the left of the dancer's body between the top two buttons (Fig. 7-19). String beads on this double thread to form the first arm (Fig. 7-20). Then, using one of the buttons you set aside for hands, thread each end of the thread through a different button hole to form a button hand (Fig. 7-21). Tie the ends of the thread and snip off the excess.

6. Repeat this last step to form the dancer's other arm, this time draping the thread from left to right (Fig. 7-22).

7. Cut another length of thread (12" to 15" long) for the legs. Thread the needle and run this thread through the loop on the bottom torso button. Lay the dancer on her back on the table and position this thread so the doll rests at its center (Fig. 7-23).

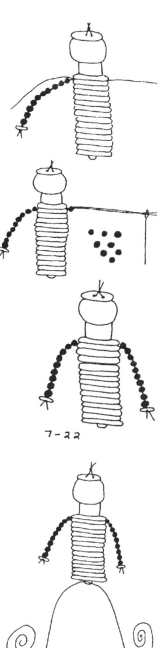

7-22

7-23

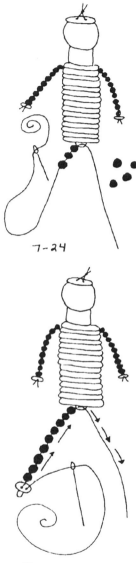

7-24

7-25

8. Thread beads onto the needle to form one leg (Fig. 7-24). Then attach one of the buttons you set aside for feet by sewing through one hole (Fig. 7-25) and doubling back through another, just as you did when you formed the dancer's torso. Continue the thread back through the leg beads and back under the thread on top of the bottom button of the dancer's torso.

9. Now you have a double length of thread on this side of the dancer's body (Fig. 7-26). Use this double length to thread on the remaining leg beads. Finally, run one segment of the thread through a hole in the remaining "foot" button and the other segment through another hole. Tie the two segments in a knot to secure the dancer's legs (Fig. 7-27).

10. Put Fray Check on all knots to prevent them from coming untied.

11. Draw or paint a face on the dancer (optional).

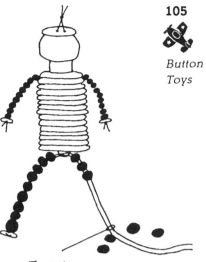

Button Toys

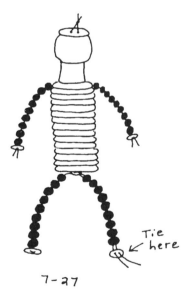

7-26

7-27

Tie here

Magical Spinning Button

Here's another quick project, and the cost of materials is practically nil. Take bets on how long you can make the button spin.

Materials

One large button (at least 1-1/2" in diameter)

Piece of string 1-1/2 yards long

Enamel paints, paint thinner, and paint brush (optional)

How to Make It

1. Paint spots of color across the center of the button (Fig. 7-28). Let the paint dry. (This step is optional.)

7-28

2. Thread the string through two of the holes in the button and tie the ends together (Fig. 7-29).

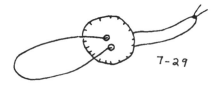

7-29

How to Play with It

1. With the button in the center of the string and your palms facing one another, hold one end of the string in one hand and the other end in the other hand.

2. To wind the magical spinning button, hold the string loosely and slip the button over and over in the air, moving your hands as though you are rowing a boat very fast (Fig. 7-30).

7-30

3. Now pull the string taut. The string will unwind and the button will spin wildly. If you then move your hands in and out (closer together and further apart), the button will spin for a long time (Fig. 7-31). Here's the magical part: If you painted spots on the button, they will turn into a madly whizzing rainbow!

7-31

MOVE HANDS IN and OUT to Spin BUTTON

A Traveler's Checkerboard

Make a portable checker game to take on car or backpacking trips. This is a fun and simple hand-sewing project to assemble before your trip. Make it along the way and later play with it on those boring "When-are-we-going-to-get-there?" stretches of highway.

The game makes a terrific present for a backpacker. You might want to consider shrinking the dimensions so the game will fit in his or her pocket.

If it gets dirty, you can wash the game board by hand in mild detergent and spread it on a terry-cloth towel to dry. Remove wrinkles with a steam iron.

Materials

Two 9" squares of red felt

One 9" square of black felt

2' of 1/8" or 1/4" black grosgrain ribbon or cord

Paper-backed fusible web, such as Pellon's Wonder-Under

Iron

12 black and 12 red buttons

Pinking shears

Sewing scissors

Red and black thread

Pins

Sewing machine or hand-sewing needle

Ruler

Fabric-marking pencil

How to Make the Game

1. Fuse the red squares together with a paper-backed fusible web (such as Pellon's Wonder-Under), then, for durability, stitch around these squares 1/2" from the edge of the fabric by machine or hand (Fig. 7-32).

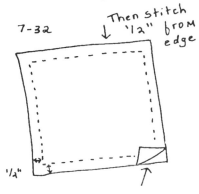

Fuse felt squares together

2. Trim seam allowance to 1/4" with pinking shears (Fig. 7-33).

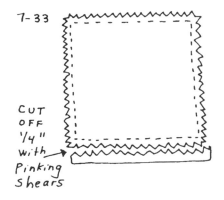

3. With an iron, attach Wonder-Under to the black felt square. Measure, mark, and cut thirty-two 1" black felt squares with sewing scissors.

4. Arrange the black squares to form a checkerboard on the red felt (Fig. 7-34). Fuse the black squares in place with an iron.

7-34

5. String the button "checkers" on ribbon or cord, roll up the game board, and tie the roll with the ribbon or cord (Fig. 7-35).

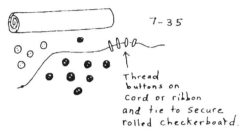

How to Play with It

Consult any standard board game book for the rules of checkers. If you're giving the game as a gift, copy these rules and include them in the package.

Tips for Using Buttons on Stuffed Animals and Dolls

Fig. 7-36 *A basket of button-eyed dolls. The sock dolls are by the author.*

Use buttons for features on dolls (Fig. 7-36 and plate 16B). A row of mother-of-pearl buttons sewn across a mouth-shaped piece of red felt makes a wonderful mouth for a rag doll (Fig. 7-37).

Buttons make fine wheels on soft vehicles (Fig. 7-38).

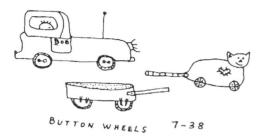

BUTTON WHEELS   7-38

Use large buttons on your next snow creation. Stick them on by inserting twigs through the holes (Fig. 7-39).

USE STICKS to Attach the buttons

7-39

Use black two-hole buttons and white thread for eyes on dolls and/or stuffed animals (Fig. 7-40).

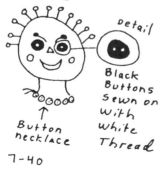

Detail

Black Buttons Sewn on with white Thread

Button necklace

7-40

Make a pair of soft dice out of red corduroy and use white buttons for the spots (Fig. 7-41).

Soft DICE For Your car's Mirror

7-41

A button sewn between the body and tail of a stuffed cat will help the tail wag smoothly. The same goes for arms, legs, and other appendages (Fig. 7-42).

7-42

A black-and-red-checked square of fabric and tiny buttons make a nice dollhouse checkerboard (Fig. 7-43).

7-43

8. Button Games

The Button Lover's Book

The first board games and game pieces were discovered by archeologists at the site of the Mesopotamian city of Ur. The game paraphernalia, which resembles Parcheesi, is believed to date between 3000 and 2500 B.C.

Costume experts do not think that the people

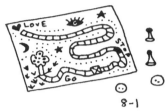

8-1

of Ur used buttons to fasten their clothes. Don't you wonder what they substituted when their game pieces got lost? At our house, we use buttons (Fig. 8-1). In fact, we often play button games. Here are some of our favorites.

Button, Button, Who's Got the Button?

8-2

If you know the origins of this traditional children's game, please write to me. Even with the help of the best reference librarians I know, I was unable to solve this mystery.

Materials

One button
Ball of kite string (optional)

How to Play It

1. Four or more players are needed; one player is "It." He or she leaves the room until asked to return.

2. The other players sit in a circle; one player sits on or holds the button.

3. The player who is "It" returns and tries to guess who has the button.

4. When he/she guesses correctly, the player who had the button becomes "It" and leaves the room.

5. In a variation on the game, "It" leaves the room and another player hides the button in a clever spot (Fig. 8-2). "It" then returns and searches for the button. The other players call out "warm" or "cold" hints until the button is found. The player who hid the button is now "It." (You might want to make rules about where the button can be hidden. "Do not move the piano," for example.)

6. In another variation of this game, players sit in a circle. One player sits in the center of the circle and is "It." The button is threaded onto a string that's long enough to go around the circle, and the string ends are tied together. Each player in the circle holds this string with both hands, palms facing the floor. Music is played while players pass the button secretly from hand to hand, all moving their hands constantly to confuse and mislead the player in the center of the circle. When the music stops, the player who is "It" tries to guess who has the button. If he or she is right, the person holding the button becomes "It" and the person who guessed correctly joins the circle.

 # Button Color Game

This is a great way to teach a toddler his or her colors.

Materials

White shoe box

Crayons

Paper scissors

Compass

Buttons in the following colors: red, blue, yellow, green, purple, orange, brown, black, and white.

Chalk or masking tape

How to Make It

1. Use a compass to draw nine circles, each 2" in diameter, on top of a white shoe box (Fig. 8-3).

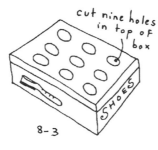

cut nine holes in top of box

8-3

2. Cut out the holes with scissors.

3. Assign a color to each hole and color a border around each hole with each of the following colors: red, blue, yellow, green, purple, orange, brown and black (Fig. 8-4). Of course, you won't need to color around the white hole.

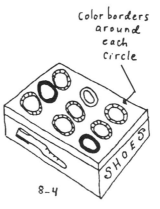

Color borders around each circle

8-4

How to Play It

You can use the color box and buttons to teach a toddler his or her colors. Red buttons go in the red hole, blue buttons in the blue hole, and so on.

Older players can use the button color game, too. Assign a number to each color. For example, red equals five points, blue equals ten points, etc. Place the button box on the floor and draw a line (with chalk or masking tape) 5' to 6' away from the box. Each player gets five buttons of each color. Players then stand on the line and pitch buttons into the holes (Fig. 8-5). A red button in the red hole equals five points, etc. The players can make up the rest of the rules. For example, a red button in the blue hole might equal minus five points. Play until someone reaches 100; then start over.

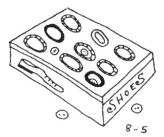

8-5

 # Button Hunt

This is a fun game for a birthday or Easter party. In fact, let's start a new tradition: button hunts instead of egg hunts.

Materials

Buttons in the following colors: red, blue, yellow, green, purple, orange, black, brown, and white (Fig. 8-6)

One large gold button

Paper bags

Whistle

Kitchen timer

Odd Fact

The buttons on designer Norma Kamali's denim clothes are all embossed with the name "Ernie." Ernie is her dog.

8-6

How to Play It

1. Hide the buttons inside or outside (Fig. 8-7).

8-7

2. Assign a number value to each color button, but don't tell the players until after the hunt is over.

3. Give each player a paper bag in which to gather buttons, then blow a whistle to signal the start of the button hunt. Set a timer. Players have one-half hour to search for buttons.

4. When the timer goes off, blow the whistle again to signify the end of the button hunt.

5. Tally up the points. The player with the most points wins. The player who found the gold button gets a special prize (Fig. 8-8).

Single Button Hunt

This is another appropriate game for a child's birthday party.

Materials

One button

How to Play It

1. Several players are needed for this game. Everyone leaves the room except the button hider.

Miss Mary Mack, mack, mack, mack.

All dressed in black, black, black, black.

With silver buttons, buttons, buttons, buttons.

Down her back, back, back, back.

—Traditional children's rhyme.

8-8

2. The button hider hides the button in plain sight but in a clever place where it blends in with the background—on the slat of a venetian blind, for example (Fig. 8-9).

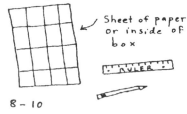

8-9

Button

3. The players return to the room and wander around searching for the button.

4. Those who spot it sit down without indicating the button's location.

5. The last person to sit down loses the round and becomes the hider for the next game.

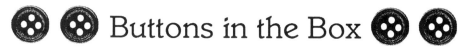

Buttons in the Box

This game is fun for all ages. Players are blindfolded, so age and experience are of little advantage.

Materials

Large flat box
Ruler
Pencil and felt-tipped pen
Button
Blindfold
Plain paper for keeping score

How to Make It

1. With a pencil and ruler, divide the bottom of the inside of the box into sixteen equal-sized rectangles or squares (Fig. 8-10).

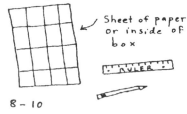

Sheet of paper
or inside of
box

RULER

8-10

2. With the felt-tipped pen, randomly number each of the sixteen rectangles or squares from 1 through 16. Assign a different number to each rectangle or square (Fig. 8-11).

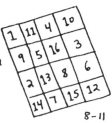

8-11

How to Play It

Two or three players are needed for this game. One player is blindfolded. That player drops the button into the box from a height of at least a foot. The numbered rectangle or square on which the button lands equals that player's points for this turn.

Another player is blindfolded, and drops the button, and so on. The first player to reach 100 wins.

Note: You can use a muffin tin instead of a box to play this game. Write numbers on the inside bottom of muffin papers, or write numbers on cardboard disks and place them in the individual cups of the muffin tin (Fig. 8-12).

8-12

Button in the Cup

This is a good rainy day game for two bored children.

Materials

Sturdy paper cup
Ball of string
Scissors
Pencil

How to Make It

1. Using the point of the pencil, punch a hole halfway up the side of the paper cup (Fig. 8-13).

2. Cut a piece of string about 14" long.

3. Push one end of the string through the hole in the paper cup. Knot the string on the inside so it won't slip out. You can tie a bead on the string or tie a fat knot (Fig. 8-14).

8-13

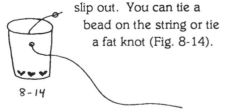

8-14

4. Tie a button on the other end of the string (Fig. 8-15).

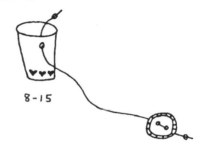

8-15

How to Play It

This game can be played as a game of individual skill, or two players can compete against each another.

The object of the game is to get the button into the cup. Hold the cup in one hand and try to flip the button into the cup without using your other hand.

Two players can take turns, scoring two points for every successful try and subtracting one point for each miss. The first person to reach thirty points is the winner. The narrower the cup, the more skill required.

Button  Pitching

This is another good birthday party game.

Materials

Chalk or masking tape
Eight buttons per play

How to Play It

1. Draw a chalk line (or mark the line with masking tape) on the floor or sidewalk parallel to and about 3' away from a wall (Fig. 8-16).

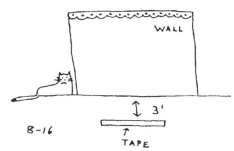

8-16

2. Players stand behind this line and take turns throwing buttons against the

wall so that they fall and land on the floor (Fig. 8-17). The object is to place

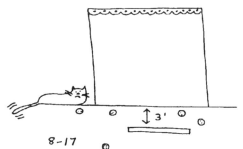

8-17

buttons as close to the wall as possible (no fair stepping over the line). If a player's button fails to hit the wall, he or she forfeits that turn.

3. After each player has pitched one button, the player whose button landed closest to the wall picks up both buttons.

4. The game is over when one player has all the buttons.

Button Knock Knock

This is another good game for a rainy day.

Materials

Two buttons

How to Play It

1. Players face each other at "shaking hands" distance apart.

2. Each player holds his or her strongest arm outstretched with the palm of the hand down and a button balanced on top of the hand (Fig. 8-18). The other hand goes behind the back.

8-18

3. Players place their "button hands" side by side. At the count of three, each player tries to knock the button from the other player's hand without dropping his or her own button. Players cannot move their feet, nor can they use their other hands.

4. The player who first knocks his or her opponent's button to the ground wins the round (Fig. 8-19). Play until someone scores twenty-five points.

8-19

Button Quiet Time

Have your child count the buttons on the clothing in a fashion magazine. Place bets on how many buttons you think there are in the magazine (Fig. 8-20).

Everyone in the family can participate in a contest to guess the number of buttons in the family button box. The person who comes closest gets to choose what to have for a special dinner (Fig. 8-21).

8-20

8-21

 Odd Fact

The button-down shirt was first worn by a British polo player; the buttons were added to keep the collar in place and out of the player's face. Brooks

Brothers introduced the shirts in the United States in the early 1900s. By the 1920s, the shirt was an accepted part of the business "uniform."

9. Choosing Buttons for Clothing

9-1   COLORED PAPERS ON FABRIC

slit

←YOUR FABRIC

Place over button on card in store

9-2   FANCY BUTTONS

BLEND IN   STAND OUT

9-3

Whether you're making a Patrick Kelly–inspired garment or your own wedding dress, one of the most important details is the buttons. To choose a button or buttons for a garment or other sewing project, lay the garment or project on a table in good light and get your button box. Now experiment by laying button after button on the garment or project. Try contrasting colors and experiment with the colors included in your fabric. If you don't have buttons in all the colors you want to try, cut scraps of colored paper and lay them on the fabric (Fig. 9-1).

If you don't have the buttons you need, carry the garment or a swatch of fabric with a slit in it to the fabric store. Insert buttons through the buttonholes or slip the fabric sample over carded buttons to see how each might look on your garment (Fig. 9-2).

Buttons can blend in with the background or have the impact of a fine piece of jewelry (Fig. 9-3). Some seamstresses prefer to choose buttons after a garment is constructed, so they can see exactly how various buttons will look. If this isn't possible, sew buttons to a scrap of your fabric with different colored threads. Put that fabric on your workroom wall for a day or two before deciding which combination you like best.

What to Consider
When Choosing Buttons

Size

Small buttons will get lost on a large coat and large, heavy buttons look ridiculous on soft, filmy fabrics. Buttons are sized by "line" or diameter measurement. Forty lines equal 1". Readily available sizes range from line 10 (very small; doll-clothes size) to line 60 (large; the size of a silver dollar) (Fig. 9-4). Button manufacturer B. Blumenthal and Com-

pany, Inc., recommends the following button sizes for garments. These are just rules of thumb, however; if a larger or smaller button looks good to you, by all means use it.

Line 18-20 (1/2") buttons for children's wear, shirts, shirt cuffs and some blouses.
Line 24 (5/8") buttons for blouses, shirtdresses, vests and jacket cuffs.
Line 30 (3/4") buttons for men's suits and leisure jackets.

Line 36 (7/8") buttons for blazers and jackets.
Line 40 (1") buttons for raincoats.
Line 45 and up (1-1/8"+) buttons for outerwear, jackets and coats.

Pay attention to the size specified on the pattern. That's the proportion the designer intended. But also use good sense. Your fabric may suggest a different size.

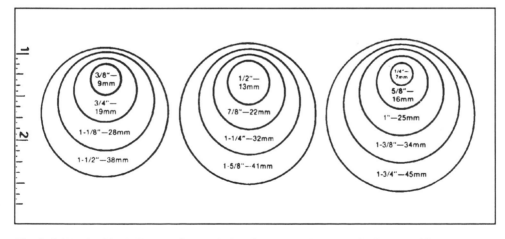

Fig. 9-4 *The La Mode Button Gauge helps determine the size of a button. Move your button from circle to circle until you find one that matches or nearly matches. Courtesy of B. Blumenthal and Company, Inc.*

Weight

Never use heavy buttons on light-weight fabric; they'll make the fabric sag. Heavy buttons and large buttons that appear heavy work best on heavy fabrics.

Care

Does the button require special cleaning? Don't use a button that can't be washed on a garment that can, and vice versa. And be sure to buy an extra button or two, no matter how expensive, in case one gets chipped, damaged or lost.

Color

Don't think you have to match the color of the buttons to the color of the fabric. Sometimes a contrasting color will give a garment the snap you need (plates 9A, 9B, and 11A; Fig. 9-5). Consider both sides of the button. Sometimes the back

9-5

side is the perfect color to enhance a garment. Shell buttons are often much more interesting on the back, where bits of the shell can add extra color to the button (Fig. 9-6). When choosing buttons for multicolored prints, look for those that

FRONT
9-6

BACK

match the darker colors or choose a combination of several colors (Fig. 9-7).

COLORFUL PRINT

9-7 USE MULTICOLORED BUTTONS

Appropriateness

Use subdued buttons on a tailored, traditional garment, such as a business suit. The buttons should blend in, rather than announce themselves. Or, as Carole Livingston, Vice President of Merchandising at San Francisco-based clothing manufacturer ACA JOE, explains, "We want our buttons to be subtle, yet enhance the clothing, while keeping within what's appropriate for the particular fabrics and styles."

Coordination

Matching the shapes or textures on a fabric with those of buttons can enhance a garment or stitchery. You may have buttons that mirror the shapes on a print fabric (Fig. 9-8). A roughly textured button may be similar to the texture of a nubby tweed. Try buttons with skinny

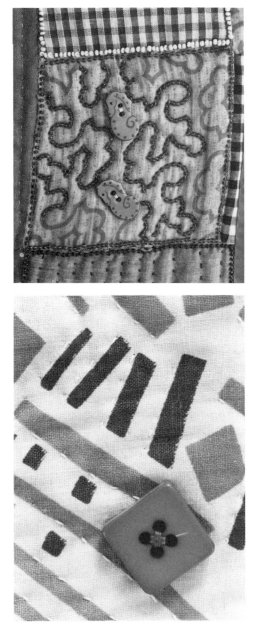

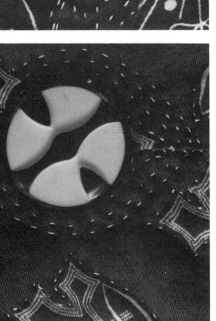

Fig. 9-8 *Buttons can enhance an unusual
print. Choose those that mirror the fabric's
design.*

stripes on fabric with wider stripes (Fig. 9-9) and play around with button

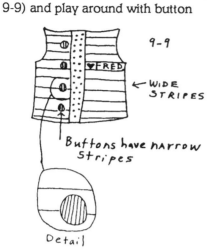

9-9

← WIDE STRIPES

Buttons have narrow stripes

Detail

placement (Fig. 9-10). You can also

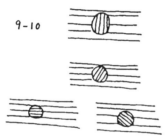

9-10

have fun with button placement on fabric with dots or checks (Fig. 9-11).

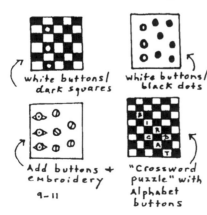

white buttons/ dark squares

white buttons/ black dots

Add buttons + embroidery

"Crossword puzzle" with Alphabet buttons

9-11

And don't be afraid to use both round and square buttons on a geometric fabric printed with circles and squares (Fig. 9-12).

9-12

BUTTONS

People with Special Needs

Large and/or rough-textured buttons are best for garments to be worn by a person with special needs, such as arthritis. These buttons are easiest to grasp and manipulate. Or use a hidden zipper to close a garment and sew nonfunctional buttons on top (Fig. 9-13). If using buttons on cuffs, sew them on with elastic so that they won't have to be unbuttoned.

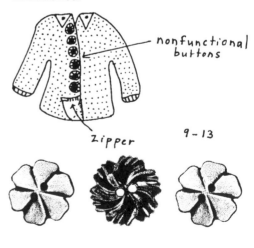

nonfunctional buttons

zipper

9-13

Creative Fashion Tips

Some seamstresses buy buttons before choosing a pattern or fabric on which to use them. A special button can serve as the inspiration for an entire outfit.

Turn a blouse you never wear into a favorite by changing the buttons. Don't think all the buttons have to be the same color or shape (plates 9A, 9B, and 11A). Los Angeles-based designers David Cline and Nina Kolarek are famous for their white blouse with different buttons down the front. The Commes des Garcons shirt collection features randomly arranged buttons (Fig. 9-14).

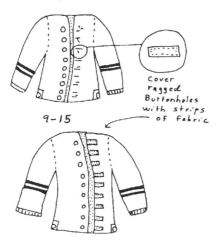

9-14

To restyle a worn garment, cover ragged buttonholes vertically with strips of fabric (Fig. 9-15) or horizontally with a wide strip of grosgrain ribbon and make new buttonholes or use snaps (Fig. 9-16).

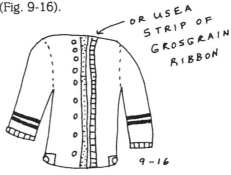

OR USE A STRIP OF GROSGRAIN RIBBON

9-16

Berkeley lace merchant Kaethe Kliot suggests replacing the top button on a blouse with a unique antique button (Fig. 9-17). "It enables you to buy one

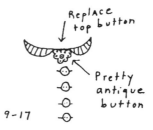

Replace top button

Pretty antique button

9-17

beautiful button for $15 or $20 and get use out of it. You can coordinate the button color with the color of the garment."

Designer Liz Claiborne often uses sets of three tiny buttons in place of one larger button on blouses (Fig. 9-18), but

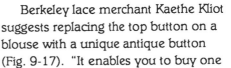

9-18

Liz Claiborne's three-button arrangement

Cover
ragged
Buttonholes
with strips
of fabric

9-15

9 - 19

9 - 20

CAROLINA HERRARA'S
TRIPLE keyhole
closure (back view)

that means more button-holes.

Buttons can enhance a dramatic angle or seam line on a garment (Fig. 9-19). Emphasize asymmetical or unusual closings with well-placed buttons. For example, consider designer Carolina Herrara's triple keyhole back closure (Fig. 9-20).

Combine ribbon, braid, and embroidered trim with buttons to create a collage blouse (Fig. 9-21). Be aware that the buttons will get in the way and prevent you from ironing the garment. However, lots of closely spaced buttons will hold most any fabric flat, so you won't ever need to iron the garment (another reason for sewing buttons on your clothes) (Fig. 9-22).

Sew rows of buttons around the top of a pair of socks or gloves (Fig. 9-23).

Small shank-type mother-of-pearl buttons look elegant around the

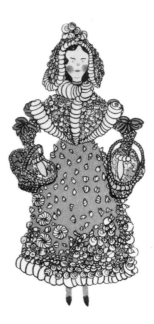

Fig. 9-22 *Buttons on clothing can make ironing difficult. But if you use enough, ironing isn't necessary.*

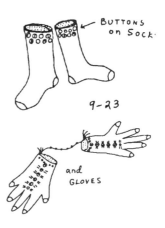

BUTTONS on SOCK

9 - 23

and GLOVES

9 - 21

edges of the collar and cuffs on a white blouse (Fig. 9-24).

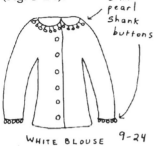

WHITE BLOUSE 9-24

Edge the hem of a black wool skirt with mother-of-pearl buttons (Fig. 9-25).

9-25 {HINT}
Pearl buttons look especially wonderful on black velvet!

A sprinkling of gold or rhinestone buttons can turn a plain, black dress into an elegant black dress.

Decorate children's sweatshirts with appliqués embellished with buttons. Draw a simple shape, such as a circle, and cover it with buttons. Some other ideas: a chocolate chip cookie with button chips, a watermelon slice with button seeds, a chocolate sundae with button sprinkles and cherry, a zoo where the animals have button eyes, an assortment of vehicles with button wheels, a button flower garden, a gum machine filled with button gum, flags with button stars, a traffic signal with buttons for lights, an apple tree with button apples, a paint box with button paints, and button awards or medallions (Fig. 9-26).

COOKIE WITH BUTTON CHIPS

WATERMELON WITH BUTTON SEEDS

STOPLIGHT WITH RED, YELLOW, AND GREEN BUTTONS

BUTTON FLOWERS

BUTTON FLAGS

red button

SUNDAE

BUTTON GUM MACHINE

USE CLEAR VINYL FOR THE GLASS

BUTTON FRUIT TREE

BUTTON PAINT BOX

BUTTON "AWARDS"

9-26

Turn a jean jacket into a showpiece by covering it with three-dimensional shapes and medallions decorated with buttons (plate 12).

Fig. 9-27 *Button-covered baseball hats are a hit with everybody, especially children.*

Cover baseball caps with buttons (Fig. 9-27). I used multicolored buttons to cover a red hat and numerous people have stopped me to ask where I got it. I used red thread and mother-of-pearl buttons to cover a black hat (it's now a very heavy hat). My aqua hat has mother-of-pearl buttons on top and delicate flower-shaped buttons around the rim.

Sew two buttons to the top of a beanie. Then make button-on ears. Depending on your mood, you or

your child can be a cat, flower garden, rabbit, or Martian (Fig. 9-28).

Buttonholes

BEANIE

Button on the ears of your choice

9-28

Did you get a free visor at last year's company picnic, but then got laid off and can't stand to look at the logo? Cover it with buttons. I even covered a heavy vinyl visor; it was surprisingly easy to sew through (Fig. 9-29).

Fig. 9-29 Buttons hide a logo on Alexander's visor. Kaitlin likes to wear her button hat backwards.

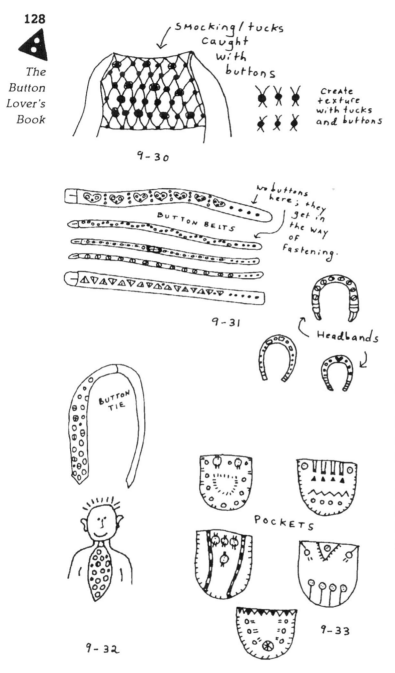

Smocking/tucks caught with buttons

Create texture with tucks and buttons

9-30

BUTTON BELTS

No buttons here; they get in the way of fastening.

9-31

Headbands

BUTTON TIE

POCKETS

9-33

9-32

When you are sewing or decorating, create texture by taking tucks in the fabric. Hold them in place with buttons (Fig. 9-30).

Cover cloth belts or padded headbands with an array of buttons (Fig. 9-31).

Make a button-studded tie for your flashy brother-in-law. Don't sew buttons to the portion of the tie that lies around the neck, nor on the part that gets knotted (Fig. 9-32).

Make button-studded pockets to sew to blouses (Fig. 9-33). These also make great presents.

Many stores now carry button covers made of metal and "jewels." Snap them over ordinary buttons to dress up a blouse or dress. For a list of mail-order sources, see Other Button Resources in the Appendices.

Have fun with checked fabrics and buttons. For example, I appliquéd a "game board" of black-and-white-checked fabric on a black sweatshirt and gave it as a gift with a box of checkers (Fig. 9-34). Fabric with dots also has possibilities.

Tassel expert Nancy Welch made a sweatshirt studded with big colored buttons. She also made tassels to match each button. Her grandchild practices his colors by matching tassels to buttons (Fig. 9-35).

9-34

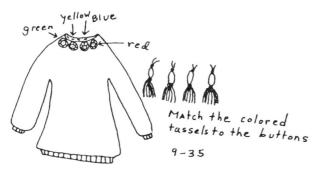

Artist Doris Hoover used ivory-colored buttons to create an effective "necklace" around the collar of a plain black sweatshirt (Fig. 9-36). Artist Pat Shipley attached a Japanese fish to her blue sweatshirt (Fig. 9-37).

Fig. 9-37 Artist Pat Shipley says she'd make the fish detachable for laundering next time.

Fig. 9-36 Artist Doris Hoover created a striking button "necklace" on a black sweatshirt.

Practical Button Tips for Clothing

Sew a button on each end of the drawstring that threads through the waistband of your sweatpants. The button will prevent the string from leaving the casing (Fig. 9-38).

9-38

Teach your child to button his or her clothing from the bottom up; the buttons are more likely to come out even at the top.

When planning a garment you will give as a gift, buy extra buttons to sew to the gift tag (Fig. 9-39).

9-39

Did you get a packet of extra buttons with your new dress? Sew them to the inside of the garment, so you'll have them with you if you lose a button. If you made the garment, keep a few extra buttons with the pattern or in your button box, sewn to a scrap of the garment fabric.

J. C. Penney's used to sell "bachelor buttons" to those who hate to sew on buttons (Fig. 9-40). If you didn't stock up, make your own. Glue shirt buttons to pierced earring posts or tie tacks to make "emergency replacement buttons" for use when you lose a button. Keep several handy in your purse (Fig. 9-41).

In an emergency,

clip here

9-41

You can clip the posts with wire cutters to make them shorter.

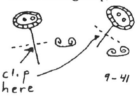

Fig. 9-40 *J. C. Penney's "Bachelor Buttons" sold for ten cents. The heavy metal buttons attach to pointed studs that anchor them to the garment.*

temporarily reattach a button with the wire from inside a twist tie. Stick the wire through the back side of the fabric, though the button and back into the garment. Twist the wire to secure the button.

Moth holes in sweaters can be "mended" by sewing buttons over them (Fig. 9-42).

with recessed centers so the thread won't be exposed to wear and tear.

If bulky buttons leave lumps on your tummy when you tuck in your blouse, consider replacing them with flat buttons. No one will see them and you'll have extra "bulkies" in case you lose one (Fig. 9-44).

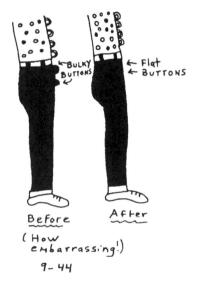

Use heavy thread to attach a button to each corner on the bottom of your favorite tote bag to create button coasters (Fig. 9-43). Choose buttons

Odd Facts

According to fashion writer Prudence Glynn, double-breasted suits were a hit because "when one side was dirty, the jacket could be buttoned up the other way." [8]

Some believe that attaching a white button with black thread or a black button with white thread will make the seamstress unpopular.

Some say that the number of buttons on a wedding dress is meaningful. For example, expect a rich groom if the bride has one or five buttons on her dress. If the gown has two or six buttons, expect a poor groom. Pity the bride with three or seven buttons on her gown for she marries a beggar.

Sewing

10. Sewing on Buttons

Button Types

There are many varieties of buttons, but only two main types. Those with an attachment with which to affix the button are known as **shank buttons** (Fig. 10-1). Shanks are most often

made of metal wire, but other materials are also used. Some buttons have shanks molded from the same material as the button (glass buttons, for ex-

ample); these are called **self-shank buttons** (Fig. 10-2). Buttons with holes

are known as **sew-through buttons** (Fig. 10-3).

Sewing on Buttons

Always begin by pressing the garment. Use thread appropriate to the weight of your fabric to attach buttons. Thread your needle before cutting the thread from the spool. Some believe this prevents tangling.

Heavier buttons can be attached with waxed dental floss or monofilament fishing line. Both fibers are very strong,

but should be used only on durable fabrics. Dental floss and fishing line can eventually cut through delicate fabrics as a garment is buttoned and unbuttoned.

In some cases you'll want to make a long thread shank instead of sewing a button tightly to the fabric. The button will lie smoothly and will not cause the fabric to pucker if you make a thread

puckering around
button sewn flat
on fabric with no
shank   10-4

shank (Fig. 10-4, without shank; Fig. 10-5, with shank). Decorative buttons,

no puckering
when a button
shank is
10-5   constructed

such as those on a jacket sleeve, do not require a thread shank.

A longer shank can be constructed with the help of a wooden match or toothpick. You set the matchstick or toothpick on top of the button before stitching and sew over it. Or use a

plastic sewing notion called a "button elevator" (Fig. 10-6), available from fabric shops or by mail (consult the Other Button Resources list in the Appendices).

Place it under the button and remove after stitching. Both methods work fine.

If you must use those "never dry-clean" buttons on the "dry-clean only" jacket you're making, B. Blumenthal and Company, Inc., has a good plan for easy button removal:

(1) Make an additional set of buttonholes where the buttons would normally be sewn. They should coincide in placement and size with the other buttonholes (Fig. 10-7).

10-6

10-7

BUTTONHOLES
WHERE
BUTTONS WOULD
NORMALLY BE
SEWN

(2) Place a strip of color-coordinated grosgrain ribbon under the buttonholes and pin the jacket front together so the buttonholes lie over one another. Mark button placement on the ribbon according to the instructions for sewing on sew-through buttons (Fig. 10-8).

Sew buttons to a piece of grosgrain ribbon 10-8

(3) Sew the buttons to the ribbon. Slip the buttons through the button-side buttonholes and secure the ribbon at the top and bottom with safety pins. To button the jacket, button the buttons through the buttonholes on the opposite side (Fig. 10-9).

BUTTON ONE SET OF BUTTONHOLES THEN THE OTHER 10-9

Sewing on Sew-Through Buttons

By Hand

Materials

Sew-through buttons (Fig. 10-10)

Sewing needle

Thread, waxed dental floss, or monofilament fishing line

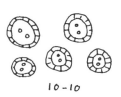

10-10

Straight pins

Beeswax

Wooden match or toothpick (or "button elevator")

Plastic tape (optional)

Fray Check, cyanoacrylate (Super Glue), or clear nail polish (optional)

How to Do It

1. Use a double strand of heavy-duty thread in a color that matches or contrasts with the color of the garment.

2. Incorrect button placement can affect the way a garment hangs, so it's important to take care in positioning them. When you sew on the buttons, begin at the top of the garment and work down. It is wise to put on the garment after attaching each button to check the placement.

To mark button placement, lay the garment on a table and pin it closed with the buttonholes over the spots

where you'll sew buttons (Fig. 10-11)

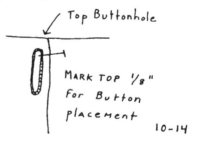

center
front

center
front

10-11

and center fronts aligned. Stick a pin through each buttonhole to mark button position. On a vertical buttonhole (parallel to the front edge), place a pin in the center (Fig. 10-12); on a horizontal

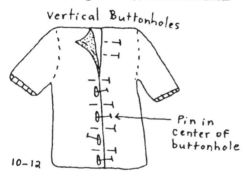

Vertical Buttonholes

Pin in
Center of
buttonhole

10-12

buttonhole (perpendicular to the front edge), place a pin 1/8" from the end closest to the edge of the garment (Fig. 10-13).

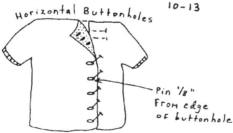

Horizontal Buttonholes

10-13

Pin 1/8"
From edge
of buttonhole

Note: Expert seamstress Claire Shaeffer recommends the following: On a garment with vertical buttonholes, place the pin at the top of the top buttonhole, so that the button shank will fill the upper 1/8" of that buttonhole. If you make a small error in the placement of other buttons in the row, this adjustment will help, and you probably won't have to remove and resew the buttons (Fig. 10-14).

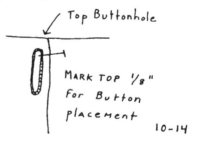

Top Buttonhole

MARK TOP 1/8"
For Button
Placement

10-14

3. Leaving the pin(s) marking button placement in the fabric, carefully unpin the garment and lift the buttonholes over the button-placement pins (Fig. 10-15). Thread your needle and knot

Lift buttonholes
carefully off
button
placement
pins

10-15

the thread. Strengthen the thread by running it through a cake of beeswax; this will also prevent knotting. Now take a stitch on the right side of the fabric at the pin's point (Fig. 10-16). Take a second stitch in the same spot.

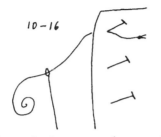

10-16

4. Using the knot as a placement guide, hold the button on the fabric or secure it temporarily with a piece of tape (if tape won't damage the fabric) (Fig. 10-17).

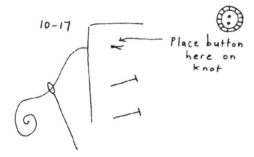

10-17

Place button here on knot

If you don't need a longer shank, there are many ways to attach a four-hole button. Almost all shirt manufacturers now use a cross-stitch to attach these buttons. Consider these other

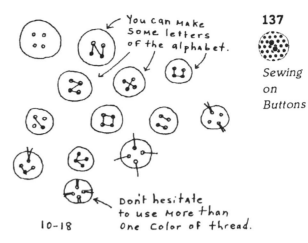

You can make some letters of the alphabet.

10-18

Don't hesitate to use more than one color of thread.

variations (Fig. 10-18). There's no rule that says you have to use only one color of thread. Some of the variations shown cannot be buttoned; use these suggestions only when a button will not be functional.

To construct a longer shank, place the wooden match or toothpick over the

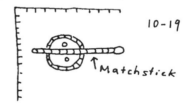

10-19

Matchstick

button (Fig. 10-19). The matchstick or toothpick should add enough height to provide a shank that measures at least the thickness of the garment. If the matchstick or toothpick does not add enough height, try a crochet hook, or use a "button elevator." Sew up through one hole, over the matchstick

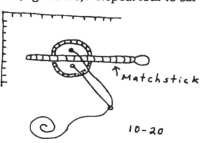

The Button Lover's Book

or toothpick, and down through another hole (Fig. 10-20). Repeat four to six

10-20

times. If you're really energetic, with four-hole buttons, sew each pair of holes with a separate piece of thread. Then if one side breaks, the other will hold the button to the fabric. End with the thread on the right side of the fabric under the button (Fig. 10-21).

10-21

5. Remove the matchstick, toothpick, or "button elevator." The button is now hanging loosely. Hold the button tightly at the top of the stitches and form a shank by winding the remaining thread around the segment that holds the button to the garment (Fig. 10-22).

10-22

Secure with backstitches into the shank. Then sew to the wrong side of the garment and knot.

6. Touch the threads on the top of the button with Fray Check, cyanoacrylate (Super Glue), or clear nail polish to add extra strength (optional).

7. Stitch a spare button or two to the inside of the garment (on a side seam, facing, or hem allowance) for emergencies.

Note: If a button has huge holes and you're attaching it to a loosely woven fabric, you don't have to use thread. For example, use thin ribbon to give the garment a romantic touch (Fig. 10-23).

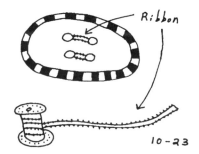

10-23

For purists: On elegant garments like tailored blazers, no thread or knots should show on the underside. Take

tiny shallow stitches and fold the fabric under the button, stitching through the fold (Fig. 10-24).

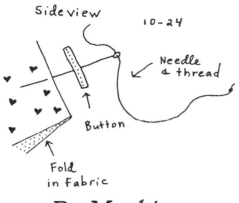

By Machine

While buttons are usually attached to fine garments by hand, buttons can be easily attached to other fabric by machine.

How to Do It

1. Thread your sewing machine and set it up for free-machine embroidery: remove presser foot, set stitch length at 0, and put feed dogs down (if possible on your machine). Decenter your needle, if possible, and put on the button foot, if you have one.

2. Mark button placement, following the instructions for sewing on sew-through buttons by hand.

3. Tape the buttons in place on the right side of the fabric. To create a longer shank, place a matchstick, a toothpick, or another sewing-machine needle on top of the button and secure with tape.

Or use a "button elevator" or a tailor-tacking foot.

4. When you sew on the buttons, begin at the top of the garment and work down. Place the needle over the button's left hole and lower the needle into it by hand. Pull up the bobbin thread and hold both threads. Lower the presser bar lever and take three stitches to lock the threads (Fig. 10-25). If your button has four holes, start with the pair closest to you.

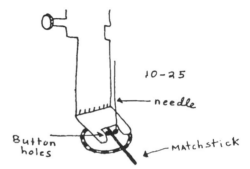

5. Adjust the width of the zigzag so the needle will stitch back and forth between the two holes. If you can't decenter the needle, you may have to move the fabric when you switch to zigzag. Then turn the flywheel by hand to check the needle clearance. Stitch

between the holes six or eight times (Fig. 10-26). Return to straight stitching and stitch several times to lock the threads.

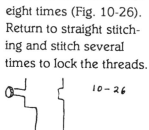

10-26

← needle

zigzag to attach button

Matchstick

If your button has four holes, move to the other set of holes and repeat

the last two steps.

6. Raise the presser bar lever and snip the top and bobbin threads (leaving long tails). It is wise to put on the garment after attaching each button to check the placement.

7. Proceed to the next button. Lower the presser bar lever and stitch another button.

8. Remove the garment from the machine. If you made a long shank,

remove the matchstick, toothpick, needle, or "button elevator." To finish, use a hand-sewing needle to thread the snipped upper thread between the right side of the fabric and the button. Wrap it around the shank several times and secure with a few stitches in the shank's core. Then pull the thread to the wrong side of the fabric and tie off. Continue this process until all buttons have been attached.

9. The final step is to remove the plastic tape.

Using Stay Buttons

A stay button, or backer button, is used to reinforce the area under a heavy sew-through button or a sew-through button on either a heavy fabric or a single layer of fabric. Use stay buttons on heavy coats and jackets and on leather, suede, vinyl, wool, and knit fabrics. The purpose of stay buttons is to reduce strain on the fabric.

Traditional stay buttons are flat, two-holed, and transparent, but any small, flat button will do (Fig. 10-27). Stay buttons

10-27

Stay Buttons

are sewn on at the same time as the primary buttons.

To sew on a stay button, place it on the wrong side

of the garment directly under a primary button (Fig. 10-28). While

10-28

Shank → ← Button

Stay Button

Fabric

holding both buttons in place, sew through both buttons according to the instructions for sewing on sew-through buttons by hand.

Sewing on Shank Buttons

Materials

SHANK BUTTONS   10-29

Shank buttons (Fig. 10-29)

Sewing needle

Thread, waxed dental floss, or monofilament fishing line

Beeswax

Wooden match or toothpick

Plastic tape (optional)

How to Do It

1. Thread the needle with a double strand of thread, waxed dental floss, or monofilament fishing line. Knot the end.

2. To mark button placement, lay the garment on a table and pin it closed with the buttonholes over the spots where you'll sew buttons. Stick a pin through each buttonhole to mark button position. On a vertical buttonhole, place a pin in the center; on a horizontal buttonhole, place a pin 1/8" from the end closest to the edge of the garment (see Figs. 10-11 through 10-14).

3. Leaving the marking pin(s) in place, unpin the garment and lift buttonholes off carefully. Thread your needle and knot the thread. To strengthen the thread and prevent knotting, run it through a cake of beeswax. Now take a stitch on the right side of the fabric at the pin's point. Take a second stitch in the same spot (see Fig. 10-16).

4. To sew the button to the garment, pass the needle and thread through the shank, then center the button over the knot. While it's not often necessary with shank buttons, you can make a longer shank by inserting a matchstick or toothpick under the existing shank (Fig. 10-30). (See the

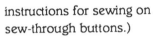

MATCHSTICK   10-30

instructions for sewing on sew-through buttons.)

If your buttons are made from a rough-textured metal that might rub against and cut the button threads, consider threading a metal eye fastener (from a hook and eye) through the button shank and sewing the eye to the fabric to hold the button in place (Fig. 10-31).

eye from hook and eye

10-31

Some shank buttons are attached to button cards with cotter pins

BACK

PEARL
BLOUSE
SET

FRONT   10-32

(Fig. 10-32). You can also use the pins to attach the buttons to the

garment. This method is often used on military uniforms so that metal buttons can be removed before cleaning. Make an eyelet (big enough for the button shank to pass through) at each button placement spot (Fig. 10-33). Insert button

Eyelets

10-33

Shank goes in hole

shanks through these holes and secure the buttons on the wrong

side of the garment with cotter pins (Fig. 10-34).

cotter pin goes here to hold button in

eyelet

Back view   10-34

5. Sew through the shank four to six times to secure the button. Secure the thread under the button with a knot or several small stitches.

Note: Shank buttons cannot be attached by machine.

Sewing Buttons on Leather Garments

Use a leather needle to attach buttons with heavy-duty thread. Always back each button with a smaller stay button or a scrap of suede on the opposite side of the fabric (Fig. 10-35). Leather and suede can tear and the extra button or suede adds strength.

Leather Button

FABRIC

10-35   Stay button

Odd Fact

Originally, all garments buttoned right to left. No one really knows for sure why men's clothing now buttons left to right and women's clothing buttons right to left. Some say the right-over-left system was easier for the maids who helped women dress and for nursing mothers. The right-to-left arrangement, however, may have been dangerous for a man who carried a sword. When a knight's garment buttoned from right to left, his sleeve could catch on his jacket when he drew his weapon. (One wonders if his surviving friends were then out to get the clothing designer.)

11. Buttonhole Alternatives

In a book about buttons, when I have so much information to share, I'm reluctant to give precious space to buttonholes, which deserve a book of their own. Therefore, this chapter contains ideas for fastening buttons without buttonholes. Refer to a good sewing manual, such as the *Reader's Digest Complete Guide to Sewing* (The Reader's Digest Association, Inc., Pleasantville, N.Y., 1976) or Claire Shaeffer's *Complete Book of Sewing Shortcuts* (Sterling, N.Y., 1981), for advice on buttonhole construction.

If you decide buttonholes will not work in a particular fabric, consider these alternatives:

Use buttons but sew snaps under them. Sew the other half of the snaps to the buttonhole side of the garment (Fig. 11-1).

Snaps

11-1

Stitch cording along the edge of the garment opposite the buttons. Leave portions of the cord unattached to slip over the buttons (Fig. 11-2). Or sew an individual elastic loop or a self-filled (or corded) tubing loop to the edge of the garment opposite each button.

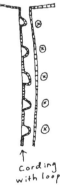

11-2 Cording with loops

Construct picot loops in place of buttonholes. Picot loops made with buttonhole stitch are suitable for delicate garments (Fig. 11-3). Make "cheater" buttonholes with iron-on tape. Determine buttonhole size, then cut patches of tape big enough to accommodate the buttonhole. You need two patches for each buttonhole.

11-3

PICOT LOOPS

Iron patches directly over and under the buttonhole site. Cut a buttonhole slit through the iron-on tape with a razor blade (Fig. 11-4). Button up.

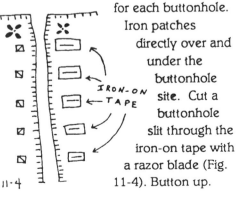

IRON-ON TAPE

11-4

You could do the same with a leather patch on top and iron-on tape underneath.

Add a seam to the center front of the garment, leaving gaps for the buttons to button through (Fig. 11-5).

Seam with gaps

11-5

Giorgio Armani garments sometimes feature a row of buttons down each side that button with figure-eight-shaped elastic loops. Make one figure-eight-shaped loop out of narrow elastic for each set of buttons (Fig. 11-6). Slip one

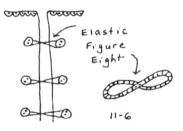

Elastic Figure Eight

11-6

end of a loop over a button on the right side of the garment and tack it to the fabric underneath (Fig. 11-7). Use the

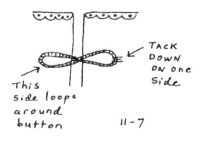

TACK DOWN ON ONE Side

This side loops around button

11-7

other side of the figure eight to button the garment.

Japanese designer Tsumori Chisato closes coats with a fitting similar to that on manila envelopes (Fig. 11-8).

Sew buttons on both sides of a vest or jacket and lace from button to button (plate 2A).

Take the garment to a dressmaker and have him or her make the buttonholes. It will cost from seventy-five cents to six dollars (the going rate in San Francisco) per buttonhole. Some dry cleaners also make buttonholes.

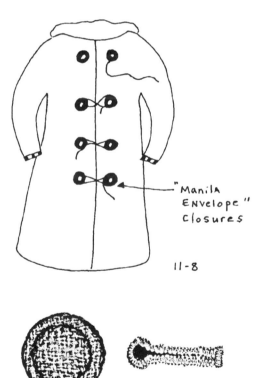

"Manila Envelope" Closures

11-8

Appendices

Odd Fact

Some consider it bad luck to wear shirts with buttons. Duke Ellington insisted on pullover shirts for that reason. He explained: "I feel that button shirts hold me in. They give me that repressed feeling." Ellington was so superstitious that he once delayed a concert for thirty-five minutes while assistants searched for a shirt with no buttons.

Identifying Button Materials

Certain button materials have distinct characteristics. If you want to learn what a button was made from, try some of the following unscientific tests. Perform the tests on the underside of the button. Be aware, however, that some collectors believe that marks made by testing reduce the value of the button. A magnifying glass or jeweler's loupe (of four- or five-power magnification) is helpful.

If you'd rather not perform a test on a button but want to identify it, contact the National Button Society to learn if there's a chapter in your area. One of the members might be able to identify your button. Don't be shy; button collectors are friendly and eager to share their knowledge. Plate 4 shows a selection of button materials and will get you started.

Bone

Bone ranges in color from white to brown. Examine the button with a magnifying glass. A bone button has a coarse, porous texture and pockmarks that resemble splinters or tiny stitches.

Glass

Place a drop of water on the button with an eyedropper. Water runs off a glass button rather than beading up. Examine the button with a magnifying glass; glass has no grain and any bubbles within the glass are round.

Horn

Rub the button briskly with your finger. Horn smells like roasting meat or burning feathers.

Ivory

Ivory has a creamy, off-white to pale yellow tone. Examine the button with a magnifying glass. Ivory's grain is distinguished by fine, curved cross-hatching. Ivory looks phosphorescent under black light.

Jet

Touch the button with a hot needle; jet smells like coal. Rub the button briskly with a cloth; rubbing should create static. Jet scratches easily and is lighter in weight than its substitutes, black glass and onyx.

Metal

Brass

Drop a small amount of nitric acid on the back of the button. If it's brass, the spot will turn green.

Gold

Have a jeweler test gold buttons for authenticity. Most jewelers have gold testing kits, also known as acid or touchstone testing kits, and will be glad to oblige.

Pewter

Touch the button with a magnet. Pewter will not magnetize.

Silver

Have a jeweler test silver buttons for authenticity. The testing process involves chemicals and is similar to that used to test gold.

Steel

Touch the button with a magnet. Steel clings to magnets. Do not immerse steel buttons in water; they will rust.

Plastic

Specific plastics are difficult to identify, as many are similar. Even experts can have a tough time making a positive determination. Identification kits featuring samples of different plastics are available, but they usually don't include older plastics such as celluloid. They also are expensive and cost $100 and up.

Bakelite (phenolic)

Phenolic plastics often yellow with age.

Touch the button with a hot needle; Bakelite smells like Lysol or carbolic acid.

Celluloid

Celluloid buttons often yellow with age. Rub the button briskly with your finger; celluloid smells like camphor (mothballs). If you touch a celluloid button with a hot needle, it hisses.

Celluloid softens when touched with acetone. Touch the back of the button with a toothpick that's been dipped in nail polish remover.

Rubber

Rubber buttons usually are black; some have reddish-brown streaks. Touch the button with a hot needle; you will smell burning rubber.

Shell

Freshwater Mother-of-Pearl

Freshwater pearl buttons are more opaque and chalky than ocean pearl buttons and do not usually have the same iridescence.

Ocean Mother-of-Pearl

Ocean pearl buttons appear iridescent.

Tortoiseshell

Rub the button briskly with your finger. Tortoiseshell smells a bit like dead fish and/or stagnant water, unlike its substitutes, celluloid and horn. **Note:** The hawksbill turtle, from which tortoiseshell was obtained, is now on the endangered species list.

Vegetable Ivory

Touch the button with a hot needle; vegetable ivory smells somewhat like burning walnut shells. Its grain is very similar to genuine ivory. As it ages, vegetable ivory sometimes deteriorates and cracks.

Button Care

If you obtain a full button box at a garage sale, chances are you'll want to sort and clean the buttons before adding them to your collection. Some buttons can be washed in a dishpan with dishwashing detergent. Others require more careful cleaning.

When I buy a full button box, I generally dump it into my largest mixing bowl and remove clinging button threads with embroidery scissors, transferring the dethreaded buttons to another big bowl. I put buttons that might get damaged by water and those that might be valuable in a third bowl. When I finish removing the threads, I dump the ordinary buttons in a dishpan, where I wash them with ordinary dishwashing soap. I spread them on clean terry-cloth towels to dry. I clean the valuable buttons and those that might be damaged by water according to the instructions that follow.

If you're in doubt about how to clean a special button, contact the National Button Society to learn if there's a chapter in your area. One of the members might be able to advise you.

For information on obtaining polishes and detergents mentioned in this section, consult Other Button Resources in the Appendices.

Antler

Antler buttons can be laundered by hand or in a washing machine. Do not soak them or use harsh detergent. Do not dry them in a hot dryer. The buttons can be dry-cleaned.

Avocado Pit

Avocado pit buttons can be laundered, but the pits can crack when washed by machine. Therefore, wash garments by hand in a mild detergent to reduce the risk of damage to your handmade buttons. Do not soak them. Do not dry them in a hot dryer. The buttons can be dry-cleaned.

Bone

Clean bone buttons with alcohol or with a non-ionic detergent such as

Orvus. Do not soak bone in water. Never use bleach to clean old bone buttons. Do not store bone buttons in extremely hot or cold temperatures or in high humidity; these conditions can cause them to warp or crack. Acid, grease, and salts can damage bone.

Ceramic

Many manufacturers of ceramic buttons recommend that the buttons be washed by hand. If you must wash a garment with ceramic buttons by machine, turn the garment inside out, so that the buttons are protected. Machine drying is not recommended because ceramic buttons can bang against the dryer and chip. If you must dry the garment by machine, button the buttons, turn the garment inside out and pin it in several places with safety pins to hold it in place while tumbling.

Ceramic buttons can be dry-cleaned, but ask the dry cleaner to "bag" the garment before cleaning to protect the buttons.

Acrylic Modeling Compound Buttons

Buttons made with acrylic modeling compound can be laundered. Manufacturers claim that the buttons can withstand machine washing. I recommend washing garments by hand in a mild detergent to reduce the risk of damage to your handmade buttons.

If your garment must be dry-cleaned, remove the buttons first. Acrylic modeling compounds can dissolve in dry-cleaning solvents.

Instructions for making these buttons appear on pages 48–52.

Baker's Clay Buttons

Buttons made with baker's clay can be laundered, but only if they've been thoroughly coated with protective lacquer or enamel. Even then, I recommend washing garments by hand in a mild detergent to reduce the risk of damage to your special buttons.

If your garment must be dry-cleaned, remove the buttons first. They will dissolve in dry-cleaning solvents.

Instructions for making these buttons appear on page 53–55.

Raku

Ceramic buttons fired with the Japanese double-firing process require special care. Wash them only by hand in mild detergent. If a garment must be dry-cleaned, remove the buttons first or cover each button with masking tape.

Fabric-Covered Buttons

Care will depend upon the fabric you select. If the fabric can take it, most "cover-your-own" buttons can be washed by hand or machine. They can also be dry-cleaned.

Glass

Wash glass buttons in water with a mild detergent. If a button is painted, before immersing the entire button, wet a small section with a damp cotton swab to be sure the paint is permanent.

Do not store glass buttons in cold rooms; glass may crack in cold temperatures.

Horn

Horn buttons can be washed in cold water. High humidity can turn them to glue. Horn is also susceptible to attack by insects. If you notice insect damage, put the buttons in a plastic bag in the freezer for several months or have the buttons fumigated.

Ivory

Clean ivory buttons with alcohol or with a non-ionic detergent such as Orvus. Do not soak ivory in water. Never use bleach to clean old ivory buttons. Do not store ivory buttons in extremely hot or cold temperatures or in high humidity; these conditions can cause them to warp or crack. Acid, grease, and salts can damage ivory. Sunlight can fade ivory.

Jet

Launder jet buttons with alcohol or with a non-ionic detergent such as Orvus. Do not expose them to extreme heat.

Knotted Buttons and Frogs

Frog buttons can be laundered. I recommend washing garments by hand in a mild detergent to reduce the risk of damage to your handmade buttons. Most frog buttons can be dry-cleaned. To be safe, ask your dry cleaner's advice.

Leather

Leather should be stored in a well-ventilated closet at room temperature. Do not store leather in plastic as lack of air circulation may lead to discoloration.

Clean spots from suede buttons with an art-gum eraser, terry-cloth towel, or soft toothbrush. Clean patent leather buttons with a mild solution of vinegar and water. Do not soak leather buttons in water.

Leather buttons can be dry-cleaned.

Metal

Antique metal buttons should be cleaned with care and never over-polished. Study this section for instructions on cleaning specific metals. Metal buttons not mentioned specifically can be cleaned in the following manner:

To remove tarnish, corrosion, or dirt from metal buttons, start by rubbing them briskly with a "blitz rag" (available at most shoe repair stores). If this doesn't work, try spraying the buttons with WD-40. Scrub the buttons with a very soft brush and/or 000 or 0000 steel wool, then rub them clean with a soft cloth. If this procedure still does not clean the buttons to your satisfaction, try polishing them with a paste polish, such as Happich Simichrome Polish, Top Brite, or Met-all Aluminum Polish. These polishes are available in hardware stores, or consult Other Button Resources in these Appendices for manufacturers' addresses.

Never store metal buttons in the same container with plastic buttons. When deprived of oxygen, some plastic buttons give off fumes that causes the plastic to deteriorate and become moist. Moisture causes rust.

If the button is sewn to a garment, cut a buttonhole-sized slit in a piece of cardboard and button the button to the cardboard before polishing the button. The cardboard will protect the fabric during polishing.

Bottle-Cap Buttons

Launder bottle-cap buttons by hand in a mild detergent. Do not wash them by machine. Do not dry them in a hot dryer.

If your garment must be dry-cleaned, remove the buttons first. The acrylic modeling compound can dissolve in dry-cleaning solvents.

Plate 13A (left) Artist Patricia Farber incorporates European metallic braids, ribbons, antique buttons, and passementerie in jewelry and accessories marketed under the name Petrushka. Her creations have appeared on television and in films; Bette Midler wore Petrushka jewelry in the movie Beaches. Photograph by the artist and courtesy of the artist.

Plate 13B (below) Here are some additional creations by Patricia Farber of San Francisco, Calif. Photograph by the artist and courtesy of the artist.

Plate 14A (above) Eight-Strand Bib *by RickaMae of Portsmouth, N.H. The artist's studio is appropriately located in an artists' cooperative called The Buttonworks. Photograph by Charles Mayer and courtesy of the artist.*

Plate 14B (left) Pin *by Ira Ono of Volcano, Hawaii. Ono combines small found treasures to create whimsical collage jewelry. He calls his wearable art the Trashface Collection. Photograph courtesy of the artist.*

Plate 15A (above) After Meeting the Monument Salesman at Talpa Graveyard *by Jane Burch Cochran of Rabbit Hash, Kentucky, 1990. Cochran, who often uses buttons on her quilts, says she "started by buying a gallon jar of buttons at a flea market for five dollars." Photograph courtesy of the artist.*

Plate 15B (right) Heart in My Hand *(5-1/2" wide by 7-1/2" high) by Marian Haigh of Austin, Texas, 1989. Haigh says she "is fascinated by non-precious materials that become valuable and meaningful to someone, that make a comment, tell a story, or just rest the soul." Photograph courtesy of the artist.*

Plate 16A *(right) Detail of Tornado I (49" wide by 48" high) by Merrill Mason of Jersey City, New Jersey, 1988. Mason uses various materials including buttons, paint, rubber stamps, photocopy transfers, metallic threads, and transparent fabrics to create one-of-a-kind wall quilts. Photograph courtesy of the artist.*

Plate 16B *(below) Medium Astrays (11" tall) by Margo Strand Jensen of Denver, Colorado, 1987. The artist claims that in a dollmaker's house buttons are known as "eyes."*

Instructions on making these buttons appear on page 71–73.

Brass

Part of an old brass button's appeal is its patina. You can use brass polish to clean the metal, but don't rub so hard that you remove that patina and destroy the button's character. Never use steel wool on brass.

Many older brass buttons were treated with a gilt, silver, or antique finish that can be damaged by even the mildest metal polish. Many collectors prefer to leave these buttons as is.

Gold

Wash gold in mild soap and water. Do not rub it with abrasive metal polish, steel wool, or cleanser.

Pewter

Polish pewter buttons with mild metal polish and a soft, lint-free cloth. If the buttons are really dirty, 0000 steel wool can be used in place of a cloth. Very heavy black tarnish must be removed professionally.

Launder garments with pewter buttons by hand or machine. They can also be dry-cleaned.

Silver

Polish silver buttons with cream of tartar and a soft, lint-free cloth. Or use a silver polishing cloth or rouge cloth. Use silver polish to remove heavy tarnish; recommended brands include Goddard's, Gorham, Haggarty's, International, or 3M. These polishes are available at hardware or jewelry stores. Do not use silver dip as it will remove the silver's patina. Rubber can damage silver, so don't string silver buttons on rubber bands.

A garment with silver buttons can be hand- or machine-washed or dry-cleaned. Turn the garment inside out before washing by machine.

Steel

See the general instructions for cleaning metal buttons. Do not immerse steel buttons in water; they rust.

Plastic

The main concern in caring for plastic buttons is water or a dryer that is too hot. Plastic buttons can melt, so be careful. Most plastic buttons can be washed by hand or machine or dry-cleaned. Poly-styrene buttons, however, dissolve in dry-cleaning solvents.

Plastic buttons should not be stored in button tins or in spaces that are poorly ventilated. Some celluloid gives off nitric fumes that can damage buttons deprived of oxygen. These fumes can make the plastic sticky or turn it to powder. In addition, the proximity of sticky plastic buttons can cause the metal buttons in your button box to rust.

If a plastic button becomes sticky, you can attempt to fix it by soaking the button in washing soda for two to three weeks. Rinse well. Then, insert a toothpick through one of its holes and coat the button with clear protective lacquer or clear nail polish. Suspend the toothpick between two bricks or shoe boxes until the protective coating is dry. Drying can take several days.

Surface scratches can be removed from Bakelite buttons with Happich Simichrome Polish.

Rhinestone

Do not immerse rhinestone-studded buttons in water, which can loosen the stones.

Rubber

Do not dry rubber buttons in a hot dryer.

Shell

Shell buttons can be laundered, but they can chip or crack in the washing machine. Therefore, wash garments by hand in a mild detergent to reduce the risk of damage to your handmade buttons. Shell buttons dyed with food coloring should always be washed by hand. Do not dry the buttons in a hot dryer.

Most shell buttons will survive dry-cleaning. To be safe, ask your dry cleaner's advice.

To clean antique mother-of-pearl buttons, coat them with WD-40 and let them sit overnight. Wipe off excess oil with a soft cloth. Buff buttons with 000 or 0000 steel wool; then polish them with a paste polish such as Top Brite or Happich Simichrome Polish. The buttons can also be cleaned with a non-ionic detergent such as Orvus.

Tortoiseshell

Wash tortoiseshell buttons by hand in a non-ionic detergent such as Orvus. Do not dry them in a hot dryer. Do not soak them in water.

Vegetable Ivory

Vegetable ivory buttons are quite durable and can be washed by hand or machine or can be dry-cleaned. As the substance ages, it sometimes cracks. If washing by machine, first button the garment and turn it inside out. Do not dry in a hot dryer. Do not soak vegetable ivory buttons; the substance softens when soaked.

Wood

Wooden buttons can be laundered. Wash garments by hand in mild detergent to reduce the risk of damage to your handmade buttons. Unfinished buttons can break in the washing machine. Those protected with clear lacquer will fare better, but the finish can deteriorate after repeated machine launderings. Do not soak wooden buttons. Do not dry them in a hot dryer.

Most wooden buttons will survive dry-cleaning. To be safe, ask your dry cleaner's advice.

High humidity and insects can damage wooden buttons. Store buttons in a clean, well-ventilated spot and inspect them regularly. If you discover insect damage, have the buttons professionally fumigated.

Button Museums

Belgium

Royal Museums of Art and History
10 Parc du Cinquantenaire
1040 Brussels
Belgium
Telephone: 011-32-02-33-96-10

Canada

University of British Columbia
Museum of Anthropology
6393 N.W. Marine Dr.
Vancouver, British Columbia V6T 1W5
Telephone: (604) 228-2974
   The museum has a collection of button blankets.

Denmark

Royal Copenhagen Museum
45, Smallegade
DK-2000 Copenhagen F
Denmark
Telephone: 011-45-31-86-48-48
   The museum has a limited collection of porcelain buttons manufactured at the facility in the late eighteenth century.

England

Bakelite Museum Society
c/o Patrick Cook
99 Blackheath Road
London SE10
England
   A private collection of Bakelite that includes buttons. Write ahead if you want to visit.

Dorset County Museum
High West St. at South St.
Dorchester
England
Telephone: 011-44-03-056-2735
   The museum owns a large collection of Dorset thread buttons.

France

Musee Carnavalet
23, rue de Sevigne
75003 Paris
France
Telephone: 011-33-42-72-21-13

Musee de la Mode et du Costume
Palais Galleria
10, Avenue Pierre Ier-de-Serbie
75116 Paris
France
Telephone: 011-33-47-20-85-83
   (near Place d'Iena and the Eiffel Tower)

Musee des Arts de la Mode
Pavillon de Marsan
111, rue de Rivoli
75991 Paris
France
Telephone: 011-33-42-60-32-14
   (near the Palais Royal Metro stop)

The Netherlands

Historisch Kostuum Museum
Utrecht
The Netherlands
   This private museum of costume and fashion features button displays. The gift shop sells antique textiles, lace, buttons, and other costume-related merchandise.

United States

Baldwin Heritage Museum
U.S. Highway 98
Elberta, AL 36530
Telephone: (205) 986-8375

Located between Mobile, Alabama, and Pensacola, Florida, this small county museum features the Bess Terry Button Collection. The collection is rich in shell and pearl buttons.

Thomas Burke Memorial Washington State Museum
University of Washington
Seattle, WA 98195
Telephone: (206) 543-5590

The museum has a collection of button blankets.

Cooper-Hewitt Museum
2 East 91st St.
New York, NY 10128-9990
Telephone: (212) 860-6868

The Cooper-Hewitt button collection is considered the best museum collection in the United States. Buttons are not always on display, so call first.

Fort Ticonderoga
Box 390
Ticonderoga, NY 12883
Telephone: (518) 585-2821

The fort has a fine collection of eighteenth-century military buttons from the Seven Years' War and the American Revolution.

Grand Rapids Public Museum
54 Jefferson, S.E.
Grand Rapids, MI 49503
Telephone: (616) 456-3973

The museum has Mrs. J. W. Rigterink's button collection on display.

Mattatuck Museum
144 West Main St.
Waterbury, CT 06702
Telephone: (203) 753-0381

The museum has a large button collection, but only a small part of it is on display. Waterbury produced many early brass buttons.

Metropolitan Museum of Art
The Costume Institute
Fifth Avenue at 82nd Street
New York, NY 10028
Telephone: (212) 879-5500

The Metropolitan Museum features buttons made for Elsa Schiaparelli by Marguerite Stix as well as other buttons of historical interest. The buttons are not always on display, so call first.

Muscatine Art Center
1314 Mulberry Ave.
Muscatine, IA 52761
Telephone: (319) 263-8282

An upstairs room contains a display on freshwater pearl button manufacturing.

Warther Carvings
331 Karl Ave.
Dover, OH 44622
Telephone: (216) 343-7513

Frieda Warther's collection of 73,000 buttons (no two alike) is displayed on the museum's walls and ceiling. A button from Mary Todd Lincoln's second inaugural ball gown was Mrs. Warther's favorite.

Button Shops

Belgium

Brussels Street Market
Vossenplein, Place du Jeu de Balle
Open every day (Mondays and rainy
days are slow) from dawn to 1 P.M.

England

The Button Box   Catalog
Mail-order address: £9.28
P.O. Box 289
London WC2E 9MA
Telephone: 011-44-71-240-2841

Shop address:
44 Bedford St.
London WC2E 9HA
Telephone: 011-44-71-240-2716

The Button Box offers a wonderful
selection of old and new buttons. Have
your checkbook ready when the catalog
arrives; it's irresistible. They also accept
VISA, American Express and
MasterCard.

The Button Queen
Mrs. Toni and Martyn Frith
19 Marylebone Lane
London W1M 5FF
Telephone: 011-44-1-935-1505

**London Badge and Button Company,
Ltd.**
Kings Meadow Lane
Higham Ferrers, Northants NN9 8LL
England
Telephone: 011-44-933-317777

Sheila Bird's Button Box
The Cottage
Nottingham, Weymouth
Dorset DT3 4BJ
England
Telephone: 011-44-305-813146

London Street Markets
Sunday: Vallance Rd. and Cheshire St.,
Whitechapel; Camden Lock Market,
Chalk Farm Rd., Camden Town;
Petticoat Lane Market, Middlesex St.
(watch for Pearly Kings and Queens).

Monday: Covent Garden.

Wednesday: Camden Passage, Islington.

Friday: Bermondsey Square, Tower
Bridge (go early); Golbourne Rd. and
Portobello Rd.; Church St. and Bell St.,
Marylebone.

Saturday: Portobello Market, Portobello
Rd. (watch for Pearly Kings and
Queens); Camden Passage, Islington;
Camden Lock, Camden Town.

France

Paris Boutons
78, rue Temple (on the Right Bank)
75003 Paris
Telephone: 011-33-1-278-01-00

Paris Flea Market
Saturday, Sunday, and Monday
"Marche aux Puces," near the Porte de
Clignancourt Metro stop.

Tissus Bouchara
54, Boulevard Haussman
75009 Paris
Telephone: 011-33-1-280-66-95

Hong Kong

Antique stores on Hollywood Road in
Central; street vendors along the steps
of Pottinger Street (near Queen's Road
Central).

United States

Button Nook at B. J. Beck's   No
Washington Ave. at Spring St.   catalog
Cedarburg, WI 53012
Telephone: (414) 375-3001

Antique buttons.

Exclusive Button Shop   No catalog
10252 San Pablo Ave.
El Cerrito, CA 94530
Telephone: (415) 524-5606

Antique and contemporary buttons.

G Street Fabrics   No catalog
Mid-Pike Plaza
11854 Rockville Pike
Rockville, MD 20852
Telephone: (301) 231-8998
　The large button and trims department is located on the upper level. G Street Fabrics also has an annual antique button show.

The Heirloom Shop   No catalog
4500 155 North
Highland Village #159
Jackson, MS 39211
Telephone: (601) 362-3602
Mail-order inquiries: (800) 451-4172
and
5002 Kingson Pike
Knoxville, TN 37919
Telephone: (615) 584-3155
　The Heirloom Shop has a nice selection of ceramic buttons; they also sell button jewelry and button jewelry kits.

JHB International Factory Outlet   No
The Backdoor   catalog
1955 South Quince St.
Denver, CO 80231
Telephone: (303) 751-8100
　This source for discontinued JHB buttons is open only to those with a resale tax license or tax exemption certificate (no exceptions). Cash and carry only.

Lacis   No button catalog
2982 Adeline St.
Berkeley, CA 94703
Telephone: (415) 843-7178
　Kaethe Kliot has a selection of

antique buttons, mostly from 1860-1900. She also has hundreds of tailoring buttons from men's clothing from the 1930s and 1940s.

P. Lipner and Co.   No catalog
208 Union, N.E.
Grand Rapids, MI 49503
Telephone: (616) 458-0075

Once Upon a Button   No catalog
Riverwalk, Space 12
New Orleans, LA 70130
Telephone: (504) 522-5992
　Owner Rose K. Magri sells antique buttons, some of which have been made into jewelry.

Renaissance Buttons   Brochure (send
826 W. Armitage   S.A.S.E.)
Chicago, IL 60614
Telephone: (312) 883-9508
　Antique buttons.

Tender Buttons   No catalog
143 East 62nd St.
New York, New York 10021
Telephone: (212) 758-7004
and
946 North Rush St.
Chicago, IL 60611
Telephone: (312) 337-7033
　Diana Epstein and Millicent Safro specialize in antique buttons. Their shops are "must-sees."

Zula Fricke's Button Shoppe   No
328 Chartres St.   catalog
New Orleans, LA 70130
Telephone: (504) 523-6557
　Antique buttons. Call first because hours are irregular.

Mail-Order Sources for Buttons

Aardvark Adventures   Catalog, $2
P.O. Box 2449
Livermore, CA 94551-0241
Telephone: (415) 443-ANTS or
(800) 388-ANTS

    Button-lover Debbie Casteel sells needlework and craft supplies. Her catalog often includes unusual buttons, as well as ideas for using them. Aardvark also stocks button-sized metal cookie cutters.

albe creations, inc.   Free brochure
2920 Century Square   (wholesale only)
Winston-Salem, NC 27106
Telephone: (919) 924-2911 or
(800) 637-0887

    Handmade ceramic buttons. Designs include cow, Easter egg, watermelon, barn, pumpkin, and more.

The Antler Works   Catalog
9100 Holland Loop
Cave Junction, OR 97523
Telephone: (503) 592-2763

    Tom Gmirkin fashions buttons out of naturally shed deer, elk, moose, and caribou antlers. Minimum order $75.

Atlanta Thread and Supply Company
695 Red Oak Rd.   Free catalog
Stockbridge, GA 30281
Telephone: (404) 389-9115 or
(800) 847-1001

    This firm sells mostly to dry cleaners, uniform rental companies, and tailoring establishments. They are a great source for ordinary buttons—coat buttons, suspender and fly buttons, uniform buttons, shirt buttons, cover-your-own buttons, etc. Discounts for large orders.

Barbara Bauer   Color brochure, $1
P.O. Box 385
Lexington, GA 30648
Telephone: (404) 743-3268

    Bauer creates porcelain buttons. Her "Orb Series" features round buttons glazed with rich colors.

Beaucoup, Inc.   Catalog
P.O. Box 1266
Greenville, MS 38701
Telephone: (601) 378-8868

    Beaucoup, Inc., sells pearl buttons. Minimum order is six dozen.

The Bee Lee Company   Catalog
Box 36108
Dallas, TX 75235-1108
Telephone: (800) 527-5271 (orders only) or (214) 351-2091

    Plastic, leather, metal, and cover-your-own buttons. Specializing in Western (as in cowboy) trims.

Blue Moon
P.O. Box 4881
Walnut Creek, CA 94596
Telephone: (415) 930-9200

    Blue Moon markets handcrafted buttons (ivory, antler, coin, porcelain, raku, wood, and fused glass). Minimum $50 first order.

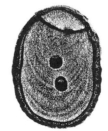

Bridals International
45 Albany St.
Cazenovia, NY 13035
Telephone: (315) 655-8500

Bridals International sells covered buttons (white or ivory) for wedding gowns.

A Bunch of Buttons   Catalog, $2
Ceramic Playhouse   (send S.A.S.E.)
420 N. Main
Grapevine, TX 76051
Telephone: (817) 488-0585

Lydia Dickerson and Peggie Sampson make ceramic buttons, many of which are available in a choice of fourteen colors. You can order the buttons in bisque at 33 percent off and glaze them yourself. Designs include stars, letters and numbers, and a wonderful hammer, saw, and pliers.

Button Hole   Free catalog
Ray and B. Travis
Route 1, Box 263-B
Madison Heights, VA 24572
Telephone: (804) 384-0539

Elegant porcelain buttons.

The Button Shop   Free catalog
P.O. Box 1065
Oak Park, IL 60304
Telephone: (312) 795-1234

A tailoring-supply business. Another great source for ordinary buttons. Tiny buttons can be hard to find and they sell some.

Buttons and Things Factory Outlet
24 Main St.   Free
Route 1   catalog
Freeport, ME 04032
Telephone: (207) 865-4480

Some people go to Freeport, Maine, to visit L. L. Bean. Button fans go to visit Buttons and Things. Best source for novelty buttons—those shaped like pandas, turtles, bears, etc.

A.G.A. Correa   Free catalog
P.O. Box 401
Wiscasset, MA 04578
Telephone: (800) 341-0788 or
(207) 882-7873

Sterling silver and fourteen-carat gold blazer buttons, "hand-enameled with your yacht club flag, private signal, or corporate logo."

The Costume Shop   Catalog, $1
P.O. Box 803
Corrales, NM 87048
Telephone: (505) 898-5020

A source for sterling and nickel silver buttons (Native American designs).

Coupeville Spinning and Weaving Shop
P.O. Box 520   Catalog, $2
15 Front St.
Coupeville, WA 98239
Telephone: (206) 678-4447 or
(800) 75WEAVE

Nice selection of Scandinavian pewter buttons, as well as antler, abalone, wood, and ceramic buttons.

Damn Yankee Pewter   Send S.A.S.E.
Derald Young   for information.
978 Wilson St.
Brewer, ME 04412
Telephone: (207) 989-7673

Pewter buttons in three motifs: Old Scottish Thistle, English Knight, and Maine Moose.

Paco Despacio　　　　Free flyer
Buttonsmith　　　　(wholesale only)
P.O. Box 261
Cave Junction, OR 97523
Telephone: (503) 592-4196

　Despacio's handcrafted buttons are works of art. Most are made from precious metals, coins, stones, and other rare or unusual materials.

Dogwood Lane　　　Catalog, $2.50
P.O. Box 145
Main St.
Dugger, IN 47848
Telephone: (812) 648-2211 or
(800) 648-2213

　Handmade and hand-painted porcelain buttons. Romantic designs.

Enterprise Art　　　Catalog, $1
P.O. Box 2918
Largo, FL 34649-2918
Telephone: (813) 536-1492

　Source for very large buttons. $.20 to $.50 each. This company also sells plastic button necklaces for $1.49. The $1 catalog price is refundable with first order.

Eugene Button Works　Free brochure
5th Street Public Market　(send S.A.S.E.)
296 E. 5th St., N.B.U. 8-6
Eugene, OR 97401
No telephone.

　Porcelain buttons that look like seashells. Available in blue or iron brown. Also sheep-shaped buttons.

Fashion Touches　　Free catalog
P.O. Box 804
Bridgeport, CT 06601
Telephone: (203) 333-7738

　Best source for custom-made covered buttons. You send them fabric; they cover buttons with it.

Fired Up　　　　Catalog, $2
192 Pilgrim Ave.　　(retail only)
Coventry, RI 02816
Telephone: (401) 823-7471

　Susan Gower makes delightful ceramic buttons. Her flower-covered hearts are especially nice.

Fresh Water Pearl Button Company
Box 40054
St. Paul, MN 55104
Telephone: (612) 698-1612

　Antique freshwater pearl buttons in white and in gorgeous color. Catalog and ten sample buttons, $6.

Barb Griffin Designs　　Catalog $1
2843 Trenton Way
Ft. Collins, CO 80526
Telephone: (303) 223-0255

　Small collection of novelty buttons.

The Hands Work　　　Send #10
P.O. Box 386　　　　S.A.S.E. for
Pecos, NM 87552　　　information
Telephone: (505) 757-6730

　Wonderful ceramic buttons. Designs range from floral hearts to Adam and Eve (complete with fig leaves). If you don't find what you need in The Hands Work's catalog, take advantage of their "Perfect Button Service." Send them a swatch of yarn or fabric and they'll make you something special at no extra charge.

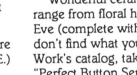

Home Sew   Free catalog
1825 W. Market St.
Bethlehem, PA 18018
Telephone: (215) 867-3833
   Good source for inexpensive buttons
for doll clothes (one gross costs $3.45).
Fifty colored lucite buttons cost $1.
Thirty novelty buttons cost $1.75.

Ladish Pearl Button Company   Free
Eastwind Trading Company   price list
417 Delaware
Kansas City, MO 64105
Telephone: (816) 474-7550
   Antique pearl buttons.

Lieber Designs   Free catalog
935 S. Rodeo Queen   (send S.A.S.E.)
Fallbrook, CA 92028
Telephone: (619) 723-5591
FAX: (619) 723-7862
   Sterling silver and brass buttons in a
variety of designs at very reasonable
prices. This company also designs
custom buttons.

Maiden Vermont   Free catalog
Danforth Pewterers
P.O. Box 828
Middlebury, VT 05753
Telephone: (802) 388-8666 or
(800) 222-3142
FAX: (802) 388-0099
   Solid pewter buttons with a cast loop
on the back. Wonderful, sophisticated
designs. These buttons are sold in
many fabric stores, but the company
also sells to individuals at retail prices.

Randy Miller Pewter Buttons
North Road
East Alstead, NH 03602
Telephone: (603) 835-2924
   Lovely handcast pewter buttons.

Janice Naibert
16590 Emory Lane
Rockville, MD 20853
Telephone: (301) 774-9252
   Mother-of-pearl buttons by the gross.
Minimum orders: one gross (at retail)
and $100 (for initial wholesale order).

Newark Dressmaker Supply   Free
Box 2448   catalog
Lehigh Valley, PA 18001
Telephone: (215) 837-7500
   Small assortment of plastic and metal
buttons, including cover-your-own
button kits. They also sell tiny buttons
for baby and doll clothes.

Yasuko Oiye   Price list
8640 N.W. Bailey   (send S.A.S.E.)
Portland, OR 97231
Telephone: (503) 286-5511
   Ceramic buttons with an Oriental
flair.

Optional Extras   Free catalog
Box 1421
150A Church St.
Burlington, VT 05402
Telephone: (802) 658-0013
   Beads and findings for making your
own buttons.

Ornamental Resources   Catalog, $15
Box 3010   (275 pages!)
1427 Miner St.
Idaho Springs, CO 80452
Telephone: (303) 567-4987
     A terrific assortment of beads and
antique buttons, Victorian black glass
buttons, and crystal buttons.

Pacific Button Company   Free catalog
2001 Emery Ave.
P.O. Box 2125
La Habra, CA 90631
Telephone: (213) 691-2200
     Tailoring supplies. Good source for
ordinary buttons.

Claribel Peacher   No catalog
6039 Remington Ave.
Carmichael, CA 95608
Telephone: (916) 961-7237
     One-of-a-kind ceramic buttons.

Poor Little Isabel's   Flyer
430 Central Ave.   (send S.A.S.E.)
Menlo Park, CA 94025
Telephone: (415) 325-3982
     Button-related products, such as
stationery, note cards, and stickers,
designed by Marilyn V. Green.

The Prairie Pedlar   Catalog, $2.50
R.R. 2
Lyons, KS 67554
Telephone: (316) 257-2937
     Antique buttons. A wonderful
Victorian button poster costs $15. Their
buttons are sold in the Smithsonian's
gift shop in Washington, D.C.

Trisha Rafferty   No catalog
Tichborne Studios
18 Tichborne St.
Brighton, East Sussex BN1 1UR
England
     Porcelain buttons (plate 8A).

Rainbow Elastic Plus   Catalog
P.O. Box 852   (send S.A.S.E.)
Solana Beach, CA 92075
Telephone: (619) 457-3950
     Abalone, conch shell and mother-of-
pearl buttons, Swarovski crystal buttons,
and striking geometric plastic buttons.
Minimum order $20.

Renaissance Buttons   Catalog
P.O. Box 273   (Wholesale only)
Oregon House, CA 95962
Telephone: (916) 692-1663
     Mary Hinrichs specializes in unusual
and old buttons. Renaissance Buttons
has a retail store in Chicago. See listing
under Button Shops.

Ridlen Manufacturing, Inc. Free catalog
4924 Reading St.
Dallas, TX 75247
Telephone: (214) 631-3660 or
(800) 445-0609
     Wholesale source for plastic buttons.
They sell large buttons (2-1/2", 2" and
1-1/2") in forty-eight colors.

Debra J. Rutherford
P.O. Box 100
Essex, MA 01929
Telephone: (508) 768-6572
     Handcrafted ceramic buttons.
Minimum order: first order, $50;
subsequent orders, $25.

Joan Denny Sample
9609 Crystal Lake Dr.
Woodinville, WA 98072
     Colorful polyform buttons (made
from FIMO).

Schoolhouse Press   Catalog
Meg Swanson   (send S.A.S.E.)
6899 Cary Bluff
Pittsville, WI 54466
Telephone: (715) 884-2799
    Knitter Meg Swanson carries Norwegian pewter buttons and clasps, as well as wooden buttons and toggles.

Sew Unique   Catalog, $1
Department MG
5656 Calyn Rd.
Baltimore, MD 21228
Telephone: (301) 744-5834
    Barbara Roberts specializes in buttons from JHB International of Denver.

The Ben Silver Corporation
149 King St.
Charleston, SC 29401
Telephone: (803) 577-4556
    Custom-designed buttons for men's blazers.

Solo Slide Fasteners   Free catalog
166 Tosca Dr.
Stoughton, MA 02072
Telephone: (800) 343-9670
    Another source for tailoring supplies and ordinary buttons.

Something Pretty   Catalog, $2.50
Route #1, Box 93
Big Sandy, TN 38221
Telephone: (901) 593-3807
    Handmade ceramic buttons.

Studio Reproduction Buttons   Catalog
Alan Faison   (send S.A.S.E.)
10 Bluebird Lane
New Braunfels, TX 78132
Telephone: (512) 629-2427
    Sterling silver buttons and pearl buttons from Bethlehem.

Tails and Yarns of Alaska   Free
Box 41   brochure
Hope, AK 99605
Telephone: (907) 782-3115
    Walrus ivory buttons and fossilized ivory buttons.

Tekison Button Company   Samples/
P.O. Box 442   price list, $4
Hailey, ID 83333
Telephone: (208) 788-3107
    Scott and Linda Schnebly make buttons from natural materials—horn, wood, antler, walnut shells, ivory, etc..

Terra Cotta Buttons   Brochure, $1
Sharon Felker
1102 Alturus
Wichita, KS 67216
Telephone: (316) 524-4578
    Another source for handmade ceramic buttons.

Tin Woodsman   Catalog
2333 Augusta St.   (send S.A.S.E.)
Eugene, OR 97403
Telephone: (503) 683-1196
    Wonderful pewter buttons.

Toledo Gold
7003 Crest Lake Dr.
Orlando, FL 38219
Telephone: (407) 351-6542
    Craftsman Mario Ballesteros makes lovely Damascene buttons—twenty-four-carat gold inlaid into steel. Ballesteros also designed and made the Damascene button .

Wildwood Works
Lasqueti Island
British Columbia
Canada VOR 2JO
Telephone: (604) 333-8881

Send S.A.S.E. for information.

Lovely handmade wooden buttons. If they don't have the color you need, Wildwood Works will custom stain buttons at your request.

Wood Forms
Foster Hill Rd.
Henniker, NH 03242
Telephone: (603) 428-7830

Product info (send S.A.S.E.)

Rosewood, bubinga, tulip, and zebrawood buttons. Highly polished and elegant.

Wooley Bear Cottage
5021 Stringtown Rd.
Evansville, IN 47711
Telephone: (812) 464-2521

Flyer (send S.A.S.E.)

Pamela Wooley purchased the entire remaining stock of circa 1900 shoe buttons from the National Shoe Company. The black shoe buttons are available in three sizes: 8mm, 9mm, and 10mm.

Worldly Goods
Audrey Ross and Allen Harrison
110 West Yankie St.
Silver City, NM 88061
Telephone: (505) 388-2122

Catalog, $3

Coin buttons, handmade African buttons, cast metal buttons (available in three finishes: bronze, copper and pewter), high-quality European plastic buttons, porcelain buttons from Scot-

163

Appendices

Odd Fact

The buttonwood tree (also called Carolina sycamore or London plane tree) grows in most temperate regions of the Northern Hemisphere. Its fruit resembles dangling ball buttons. Its wood is popular for furniture and has also been used for buttons. Speaking of button trees, the small town of Buttonwillow, California, was named for one (California Historical Landmark No. 492). Local residents dubbed the ancient tree "buttonwillow" because its dangling seedpods resemble ball buttons.

Other Button Resources

Acrylic Modeling Compounds

AMACO
Consumer Products Division
4717 W. Sixteenth St.
Indianapolis, IN 46222
Telephone: (317) 244-6871 or
(800) 428-3239
    AMACO imports FIMO and supplies it to retailers in the U.S. Call them to learn where FIMO is sold in your area.

The Clay Factory of Escondido
P.O. Box 1270
Escondido, CA 92033-1270
Telephone: (619) 741-3242 or
(800) 243-3466
    Brochure (send #10 S.A.S.E.)
    Mail-order supplier of FIMO and Cernit modeling materials. They also sell a wonderful selection of button-sized metal cookie cutters.

Eberhard Faber GmbH
Postfach 1220
D-8430 Neumarkt
West Germany
    Manufacturer of FIMO acrylic modeling compound.

Polyform Products Company
P.O. Box 2119   Catalog, $1
Schiller Park, IL 60176
Telephone: (312) 678-4836
    Manufacturer of Sculpey III and PRO/ MAT II acrylic modeling compounds.

TSI, Inc.   Free catalog
101 Nickerson St.
P.O. Box 9266
Seattle, WA 98109
Telephone: (206) 282-3040 or
(800) 426-9984 (outside of Washington)
    Great selection of FIMO.

Acrylic Sheet

Tap Plastics
3119 Mission Street
San Francisco, CA 94110
Telephone: (415) 821-7060

Antler

Jackson Hole Antler Auction
Jackson Hole Visitors' Council
Jackson, Wyoming 83001
Telephone: (800) 782-0011
    Jackson's Boy Scout Troop 200 sponsors the only regular auction of elk antlers in the U.S. It takes place on the third Saturday in May. In 1989 the going price was $15/pound. Contact the Jackson Hole Visitors' Council for more information.

Baseball Caps

Dharma Trading Company Free catalog
P.O. Box 916
San Rafael, CA 94915
Telephone: (800) 542-5227 or
(415) 456-7657
   White 100 percent cotton sun visors
and cotton twill or nylon baseball caps
for decorating and/or dyeing. Low
prices.

Button Boxes

Craft Catalog Catalog, $2
6095 McNaughton Centre
Columbus, OH 43232
Telephone: (800) 777-1442
   Craft Catalog sells a variety of
unfinished bentwood boxes and papier-
mâché boxes at very reasonable prices.

Nancy's Notions Free catalog
333 Beichl Ave.
P.O. Box 683
Beaver Dam, WI 53916
Telephone: (414) 887-0690
   Make your own heart-shaped box
with Nancy's kits.

Shaker Workshops Free catalog
P.O. Box 1028
Concord, MA 01742
Telephone: (617) 648-8217
   The Shaker Workshops sell some of
the nicest button boxes I've seen.
They're ideal for buttons because they're
not airtight. The boxes are handmade
of high-quality woods and held together
with brass tacks. Boxes are available
finished or unfinished.

TALAS Division
Technical Library Service, Inc.
213 W. 35th St.
New York, NY 10001
Telephone: (212) 736-7744
   Acid-free storage boxes.

University Products, Inc. Free catalog
P.O. Box 101
Holyoke, MA 01041-0101
Telephone: (800) 628-1912 (orders),
(800) 762-1165 (questions), or
(800) 336-4847 (for calls within
Massachusetts)
   Acid-free storage boxes.

Button-Covering Kits

Atlanta Thread and Supply Company
695 Red Oak Rd. Free catalog
Stockbridge, GA 30281
Telephone: (404) 389-9115 or
(800) 847-1001

Maxant Button and Supply Company
117 S. Morgan St.
Chicago, IL 60607
Telephone: (312) 226-7545

Newark Dressmaker Supply
6273 Ruch Rd. Free catalog
P.O. Box 2448
Lehigh Valley, PA 18001
Telephone: (215) 837-7500

William Prym, Inc.
Dayville, CT 06241
Telephone: (203) 774-9671

Risdon Corporation
Sewing Notions Division
P.O. Box 5028
Spartanburg, SC 29304
Telephone: (803) 576-5050

Button Covers

Eddie Bauer   Free catalog
Fifth and Union
P.O. Box 3700
Seattle, WA 98124-3700
Telephone: (800) 426-8020,
(800) 462-6757 (TDD for those who are
hearing-impaired), or (206) 641-2564

HHH Enterprises
P.O. Box 487
Abilene, TX 79604-0487
Telephone: (800) 444-0449

Charles Keath, Ltd.   Free catalog
1265 Oakbrook Dr.
Norcross, GA 30093
Telephone: (800) 388-6565

Krumark Industries   Send S.A.S.E. for
439 E. 82nd St.   information
New York, NY 10028-8078
Telephone: (212) 288-1470

New Mexico Catalog   Free catalog
1700 Shalem Colony Trail
P.O. Box 261
Fairacres, NM 88033-0261
Telephone: (800) 678-0585

Sundance   Free catalog
780 W. Layton Ave.
Salt Lake City, UT 84104
Telephone: (800) 422-2770

Button Elevator

Clotilde, Inc.   Catalog, $2
1909 S.W. First Ave.
Fort Lauderdale, FL 33315-2100
Telephone: (305) 761-8655

Nancy's Notions   Free catalog
333 Beichl Ave.
P.O. Box 683
Beaver Dam, WI 53916
Telephone: (414) 887-0690

The Perfect Notion   Catalog, $1
566 Hoyt St.
Darien, CT 06820
Telephone: (203) 968-1257
    You glue the buttons of your choice
to the Perfect Notion's button covers.
They suggest making several sets and
changing them "to make a plain blouse
exactly match three different skirts."

Richard the Thread   Catalog, $1
8320 Melrose Ave., #201
Los Angeles, CA 90069
Telephone: (800) 621-0849, ext. 226,
or (213) 852-4997

Button Jewelry

Antiquewear
Jerry Fine
82-84 Front St.
Marblehead, MA 01945
Telephone: (617) 631-4659

Jerry Fine converts antique buttons into rings, cuff links, tie tacks, pendants, brooches, pins, and/or earrings. Write with your request and send a S.A.S.E. for a reply.

Earlooms: Jewelry from Vintage Buttons
No catalog
P.O. Box 1216
Mandeville, LA 70448
Telephone: (504) 626-7304

Earrings and pins made from antique buttons.

Grandmother's Buttons
No catalog
P.O. Box 1689
140 Ferdinand St.
St. Francisville, LA 70775
Telephone: (504) 635-4107

Jewelry made from vintage buttons.

Linda Newman
506 S. Westland, #7
Tampa, FL 33606
Telephone: (813) 251-0870

Collage pins from antique frames, photos, buttons, and trinkets.

Olde Button Ears
Unique Jewelry from Heirloom Buttons
Berry and Jacque Negrotto
4438 Orleans Ave.
New Orleans, LA 70119
Telephone: (504) 488-6926

Berry and Jacque travel all over the world in search of buttons for the jewelry they make in their home studio.

They sell the jewelry at craft shows throughout the United States. They also do custom work for those who want to use special buttons. Prices start at $20. Write with your request and send a S.A.S.E. for a reply.

Ira Ono Designs
P.O. Box 112
Volcano, HI 96785
Telephone: (808) 967-7261

Collage pins, hair ornaments, and masks.

Sheila Schiller
No catalog
Vintage Vanities
1145 Thorn Hill Lane
Highland Park, IL 60035
Telephone: (708) 432-0644

Schiller makes jewelry from antique buttons, most dating from 1850-1900 and 1910-1940.

Cookie Cutters, Button-Size

Aardvark Adventures
Catalog, $2
P.O. Box 2449
Livermore, CA 94551-0241
Telephone: (415) 443-ANTS (information) or (800) 388-ANTS (orders)

Four different 5/16" cutters (circle, flower, petal, and heart), $1.69 each.

The Clay Factory of Escondido
P.O. Box 1270
Escondido, CA 92033-1270
Telephone: (619) 741-3242 or (800) 243-3466

Send #10 S.A.S.E. for brochure.

A Cook's Wares   Catalog, $2
West Mayfield Boro
37th and W. 3rd Ave.
Beaver Falls, PA 15010-2103
Telephone: (412) 846-9490
    Set of 12 minicutters, $9.

Poor Little Isabel's   Send #10 S.A.S.E.
430 Central Ave.   for brochure
Menlo Park, CA 94025
Telephone: (415) 325-3982

Game Pieces

Meisel Handware Specialties
P.O. Box 70   Catalog, $1
Mound, MN 55364-0070
Telephone: (800) 441-9870
    Plastic game pieces, wooden check-
ers, letters, and turnings for making
buttons.

Jewelry Findings

The Button Shop   Free catalog
P.O. Box 1065
Oak Park, IL 60304
Telephone: (312) 795-1234

Clotilde, Inc.   Catalog, $2
1909 S.W. First Ave.
Fort Lauderdale, FL 33315-2100
Telephone: (305) 761-8655

Fire Mountain Gems and Findings
28195 Redwood Highway   Catalog, $2
Cave Junction, OR 97523
Telephone: (503) 592-2222

Newark Dressmaker Supply
6273 Ruch Road   Free catalog
P.O. Box 2448
Lehigh Valley, PA 18001
Telephone: (215) 837-7500

The Perfect Notion   Catalog, $1
566 Hoyt St.
Darien, CT 06820
Telephone: (203) 968-1257

TSI, Inc.   Free catalog
101 Nickerson St.
P.O. Box 9266
Seattle, WA 98109
Telephone: (206) 282-3040 or
(800) 426-9984 (outside of Washington)

Jewelry Tools

TSI, Inc.   Free catalog
101 Nickerson St.
P.O. Box 9266
Seattle, WA 98109
Telephone: (206) 282-3040 or
(800) 426-9984 (outside of Washington)

Leather

Horizon Leather Company
38 West 32nd St.
New York, NY 10001
Telephone: (212) 564-1886

Tandy Leather Company   Free catalog
P.O. Box 791
Fort Worth, TX 76101
Telephone: (817) 551-9779

Magnifying Glasses and Loupes

University Products, Inc.   Free catalog
P.O. Box 101
Holyoke, MA 01041-0101
Telephone: (800) 628-1912 (orders),
(800) 762-1165 (questions), or
(800) 336-4847 (for calls within Massachusetts)

Metal Polish

Competition Chemicals, Inc.
P.O. Box 520
Iowa Falls, IA 50126
Telephone: (515) 648-5121
   Imports Happich Simichrome Polish from Germany.

J. Goddard and Sons
c/o Northern Laboratories, Inc.
Box 803
Manitowoc, WI 54220
Telephone: (414) 684-7137

Orvus Non-Ionic Detergent

Clotilde, Inc.   Catalog, $2
1909 S.W. First Ave.
Fort Lauderdale, FL 33315-2100
Telephone: (305) 761-8655

Proctor and Gamble
One North Charles St.
Baltimore, MD 21201
Telephone: (301) 576-5616

Glossary of Colorful Button Terms

Aristocrat—A black glass button with an incised design.

Ball—A globe-shaped, spherical button.

Bezel—The metal rim that holds the stone in place, as in a ring.

Birdcage—A shank that looks like a birdcage.

Bull's eye—A shank button with a ring or rings and a dot in the center.

Covered button—A button made by covering a button mold with fabric, leather, or stitches.

Cricket cage—A spherical, hollow button made of filigree.

Damascene button—A steel button inlaid with precious metals such as gold and silver.

Diminutive—A very small button.

Drum—A drum-shaped button.

Escutcheon—A metal shape on the face of a button.

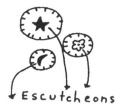

Fish eye—A sew-through button whose holes are set in a recess shaped like a fish.

Fluted button—A button with a fluted border, sometimes called a "piecrust button."

Goofy—See **Realistic.**

Habitat—A button with botanical or zoological specimens mounted under glass.

Memory button—A rare Victorian glass button containing a lock of hair, sometimes called "hair button."

Netsuke—A Japanese carved toggle used to fasten a small purse to a kimono sash.

Passementerie—Fancy eighteenth-century trimmings made of braid, beads, metallic threads, sequins, and so forth.

Raindrops—Small bubbles in glass buttons. Buttons with lots of raindrops are called "snowstorms."

Realistic—A button in the shape of an actual object, such as a cat or cow.

Reflector—A glass button with paint or colored foil between the glass and the base.

Self-shank button—A button made in one piece with a hole through a protrusion on the back.

Sew-through button—A button with holes pierced through it.

Shank button—A button with a U-shaped loop (usually made of metal) on the back.

Shirt button—A small mother-of-pearl or synthetic button with four holes and a ridge around the circumference.

Sporting button—A button featuring a sporting scene, such as horseback riding.

Talisman button—A button worn for good luck.

Toggle—An oblong button usually of wood or leather attached to a dangling loop on one side of a garment and buttoned through a similar loop on the opposite side.

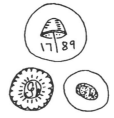

Underpainting—Painting on the underside of glass.

Washington Inaugural buttons—Made for delegates to George Washington's first and second inaugurations, these buttons are among the most valuable buttons to collectors. Twenty-two different designs exist.

Odd Fact

The origin of the police nickname "cop" or "copper" is uncertain, but some believe it derives from the large copper buttons worn by London bobbies in the nineteenth century.

Bibliography

Button Blankets

Arts and Crafts of the Northwest Coast Indians and the Eskimos. Washington, D.C.: Office of Public Information, Department of Anthropology, National Museum of Natural History, Smithsonian Institution, 1988. (Bibliography)

Bancroft-Hunt, Norman. *People of the Totem*. New York: G. P. Putnam's Sons, 1979.

Dyal, Susan. *Preserving Traditional Arts: A Toolkit for Native American Communities*. Los Angeles: The American Indian Studies Center, University of California, 1985.

Gunther, Erna. *Art in the Life of the Northwest Coast Indians*. Portland, Ore.: Portland Art Museum, 1966.

Jensen, Doreen, and Sargent, Polly. *Robes of Power: Totem Poles on Cloth*. Vancouver: University of British Columbia Press, 1986.

Buttons, Ceramic

Dustin, Kathleen. "The Use of Polyform in Bead-Making." *Ornament*, Spring 1988, pp. 17-19.

Hollman, Ursula. *Modelling with FIMO*. West Germany: Adolph Thiemann GmbH and Co., 1984.

McLanathan, Richard. *The Art of Marquerite Stix*. New York: Harry N. Abrams, 1977.

McNeill, Suzanne. *Colored Clay Mates Easy Jewelry* (Pamphlet 2085). Fort Worth: Design Originals, 1989.

New FIMO Modelling Ideas. West Germany: Eberhard Faber GmbH, 1986.

Wan, Linda. *High Fashion Jewelry Through the Art of Sculpey*. Schiller Park, Ill.: Polyform Products Co., 1989.

Buttons, General

Albert, Lillian Smith, and Kent, Kathryn (pseud.). *The Complete Button Book*. Garden City, N.Y.: Doubleday and Co., 1949.

Anderson, Joseph, ed. *The Town and City of Waterbury, Connecticut*, Volumes 1 and 2. New Haven: Price and Lee Company, 1896, pp. 275-278.

Brown, Dorothy Foster. *Button Parade*. Chicago: Lightner Publishing Co., 1942.

Cherkofsky, Naomi. "Grandmother's Button Jar." *Woman's Day*, March 10, 1981.

Clement, Joyce. *The Official Price Guide to Sewing Collectibles*. New York: The House of Collectibles, 1987.

Couse, L. Edwina, and Maple, Marguerite. *Button Classics*. Chicago: Lightner Publishing Co., 1941.

Dauterman, Carl C. *Buttons in the Collection of the Cooper-Hewitt Museum* (catalog for "Button, Button" exhibition). Washington, D.C.: The Smithsonian Institution, 1982.

Deming, Phyllis B., ed. *A History of Williamsburg in Massachusetts.* Williamsburg, Mass.: 1946, pp. 256-259.

Epstein, Diana. *A Collector's Guide to Buttons.* New York: Walker and Co., 1990.

Ertell, Viviane Beck. *The Colorful World of Buttons.* Princeton: The Pyne Press, 1973.

Ford, Grace Horney. *The Button Collector's History.* Springfield, Mass.: Pond-Ekberg Co., 1943.

Graham, Elinor. *Maine Charm String.* New York: Macmillan, 1946.

Hughes, Elizabeth, and Lester, Marion. *The Big Book of Buttons.* Sedgwick, Me.: New Leaf Publishers, 1991. (Address: 50 Benjamin River Rd., Sedgwick, ME 04676-9729)

Hutchings, Margaret. *Button-Box Book.* Central Islip, N.Y.: Transatlantic Arts, Inc., 1976.

Luscomb, Sally C. *The Collector's Encyclopedia of Buttons.* New York: Crown Publishers, Inc., 1967.

Luscomb, Sally C., and Cassidy, Ethel. *The Old Button Box.* Southington, Conn.: Quiz Industries, 1951.

National Button Bulletin. National Button Society (2733 Juno Place, Akron, OH 44313), $15/year.

Olson, Lorraine. *Old Buttons and Their Values.* Chicago: Lightner Publishing Co., 1940.

Peacock, Primrose. *Antique Buttons: Their History and How to Collect Them.* New York: Drake Publishing, 1972.

Peacock, Primrose. *Discovering Old Buttons.* London: Shire Publications, Ltd., 1978.

Schiff, Stefan O. *Buttons: Art in Miniature.* Berkeley: Lancaster-Miller Publishers, 1980.

Shull, Thelma. *The Button String.* Chicago: Lightner Publishing Co., 1942.

Van Court, Don. *Transportation Uniform Buttons —Volume 1: Railroads.* Self-published (41 Hillcrest Rd., Madison, NJ 07940), 1990. (Van Court is working on volume 2, which will cover buttons from transportation authorities, interurban lines, city transit companies, and bus and truck lines.)

Buttons, Pearl

Coker, R. E. "Freshwater Mussels and Mussel Industry of the United States," *Bureau of Fisheries Bulletin,* vol. 36. Washington, D.C.: U.S. Department of Commerce, 1919.

Farrel-Beck, Jane, and Meints, Rebecca. "The Role of Technology in the Freshwater Pearl Button Industry of Muscatine, Iowa, 1891–1910." *Annals of Iowa 47,* Summer 1983, pp. 1-18.

Madson, John. *Up on the River.* New York: Schocken Books, 1985.

Scarpino, Philip. *Great River: An Environmental History of the Upper Mississippi, 1890-1950.* Columbia, Mo.: University of Missouri Press, 1985.

White, D. P. "The Birmingham Button Industry." *Post Medieval Archeology*, vol. 2, London, 1977.

Buttons, Plastic

Katz, Sylvia. *Plastics: Common Objects, Classic Designs*. New York: Harry N. Abrams, 1984.

Costume

Binder, Pearl. *The Pearlies*. London: Jupiter Books, 1975.

Cunningham, Phyllis, and Lucas, Catherine. *Costume for Births, Marriages and Deaths*. New York: Barnes and Noble Book, 1972.

Dar, S. N. *Costumes of India and Pakistan: A Historical and Cultural Study*. Bombay: D. B. Taraporevala Sons and Co. Private Ltd., 1969.

Earle, Alice Morse. *Two Centuries of Costume in America, MDCXX–MDCCCXX*. New York: Macmillan, 1910.

Fisher, Angela. *Africa Adorned*. New York: Harry N. Abrams, Inc., 1984.

Fox, Lilla Margaret. *Folk Costume of Eastern Europe*. London: Chatto and Windus, 1977.

Fox, Lilla Margaret. *Folk Costume of Southern Europe*. Boston: Plays, Inc., 1972.

Fox, Lilla Margaret. *Folk Costume of Western Europe*. London: Chatto, Boyd and Oliver, 1969.

Hiler, Hilaire. *From Nudity to Raiment: An Introduction to the Study of Costume*. New York: F. Weyhe, 1929.

Holme, Charles, ed. *Peasant Art in Sweden, Lapland and Iceland*. London: The Studio, Ltd., 1910.

Lester, Katherine Morris, and Kerr, Rose Netzorg. *Historic Costume: A Resume of Style and Fashion from Remote Times to the Nineteen-Seventies*. Peoria, Ill.: Charles A. Bennett Co., Inc., 1977.

Levin, M. G., and Potapov, L. P. *The Peoples of Siberia*. Chicago: University of Chicago Press, 1964.

Nevison, J. L. "Buttons and Buttonholes in the Fourteenth Century." *Costume—The Journal of the Costume Society*, no. 11 (1977), pp. 38-44.

Onassis, Jacqueline, ed. *In the Russian Style*. New York: Viking Press, 1976.

Peacock, Primrose. "Buttons on the Dress of Household Servants." *Costume—The Journal of the Costume Society*, no. 13 (1979), pp. 54-57.

Petterson, Carmen L. *The Maya of Guatemala: Their Life and Dress*. Seattle: University of Washington Press, 1976.

Rhodes, Zandra, and Knight, Anne. *The Art of Zandra Rhodes*. Boston: Houghton Mifflin Co., 1985.

Russian Folk Clothing from the Collection of the State Ethnographical Museum of the People of the U.S.S.R. U.S.S.R.: Khudoznik RSFSR Publishers, 1984.

Schiaparelli, Elsa. *Shocking Life*. New York: E. P. Dutton, 1954.

Schwebke, Phyllis W., and Krohn, Margaret B. *How to Sew Leather, Suede, Fur*. New York: The Bruce Publishing Co., 1970.

Snowden, James. *The Folk Dress of Europe*. New York: Mayflower Books, 1979.

Weir, Shelagh. *Palestinian Costume*. Austin: University of Texas Press, 1989.

Gwinnett, Button

Jenkins, Charles Francis. *Button Gwinnett Signer of the Declaration of Independence*. Garden City, N.Y.: Doubleday, Page and Co., 1926.

The author and her nephew, Mitchell Green, found this button in Grand Rapids, Michigan. "Lorrie's Button" by Hy Zelkowitz was given to the children of Grand Rapids by the Arts Council of Greater Grand Rapids, MI, July 6, 1976. If you find a button treasure or have a button story to share, please write to the author at 430 Central Avenue, Menlo Park, CA 94025.

Button Box Memories

Here are some friends' button box memories. I'd also like to hear yours, so please write to me.

"A button box is one of the few things I have from my grandmother—Nana. When I was small, I played with it frequently. All the buttons were jumbled together and I would pick out my favorites and see how many I could find.

"Now that I'm grown up, I have put all the same ones together and strung them on thread. The special ones I put in a plastic box that was in with the buttons. For two years now I have been wanting to make a button bracelet out of them. They are still special to me, so I want to use them in a special way." —Vicki L. Johnson, artist (Soquel, Calif.)

"My mother didn't keep buttons in a box, but rather a jar. It is very humid in Indiana and the jar kept the buttons nicely. In fact, when my father passed away recently, I took my mom's button jar. I tossed the dirty old jar but kept all the buttons.

"Mom would snip the buttons off anything being recycled as a rag—old shirts, blouses, dresses, and so on.

"One fun use of the button jar was on December 24 late at night when all were awaiting Santa Claus. My oldest brother would climb on the back porch and stomp around (reindeer), shake the button jar (in lieu of bells) and yell 'Merry Christmas.' We'd jump out of bed and run downstairs to see what Santa had brought us." —Katy Obringer, children's librarian (Saratoga, Calif.)

"When my children were very small, ages two and four, a wonderful neighborhood lady used to 'sit' with them. They liked going to spend the afternoon at Mrs. Costa's, because she let them play with her buttons, which she kept in a coffee can. She always expressed interest in my sewing projects and stitchery. When she died, her husband gave me her button can. It was filled with treasures, which I've used with joy. For example, I've just used **again** some of her bone buttons on a jacket." —Julia Borne, fabric artist (Sunnyvale, Calif.)

"The button box I remember belonged to my grandmother's sister. We lived in the country and to get to her house we marched across fields. I was three or four years old—those are my last memories of her. She had a button tin with pictures on it. She let me play with the buttons if I'd promise to pick them all up. I would line them up and make a train through the house. The fun was in the variety—buttons of all colors and sizes. I don't have any of her buttons, but I do have bowls full of buttons in my home. I love to run my hand through the buttons. Buttons have an emotional attachment." —Clydine Peterson, artist (Menlo Park, Calif.)

"One day Scott came home from school and asked his mom if he could have some buttons from her button box to take to school for a project. Debbie told him she didn't have a button box, but if he would find out what kind of buttons were needed, she would buy some for him.

"The capper to this story is that Scott came home from school and reported, 'The teacher says all *good* mothers have button boxes!'

"Remember, this is the message Scott received. This may not have been literally what was said, but for quite a few days (before she could see the funny side of it) buttons were a very tender subject to discuss with Deb. She didn't have a button box because by the time the buttons fall off or otherwise become eligible for membership in a button box, the garment attached thereto is so worn, it is tossed out. Deb not only doesn't 'do' ironing, she doesn't 'do' sewing on buttons.

"So a friend came to the rescue. Margo mailed Deb a glorious, real button box. It is eight-sided, has a fitted lid, and the message on the bottom reads, 'Debbie's Button Box. Presented 11/20/86 to Deborah in the interest of her emotional stability and to assure the fact that she will be a good mother.'

"Inside the box was a sheet of paper and attached to the sheet was a series of buttons, each with a label. The labels read, 'Susan's Kindergarten Coat,' 'Steve's Size 7 Blazer,' 'Grandma Ladman's Dress,' and so on.

"The last item Margo included in the button box was a marble. Margo wrote, 'Button boxes can also hold broken jewelry, small gold pins, and marbles. Here is one I lost a long time ago. I donate it to help replace the ones YOU have lost!'" —Jerry Zarbaugh, founder of Aardvark Adventures (Livermore, Calif.)

"After the article appeared I started to receive buttons. I now have three tins full of buttons. Some are antique, some are one-of-a-kind buttons, some are handmade, and some are just plain strange. It's great. Of course, you realize, there is not a button in the bunch I would let go to school for 'button math.' They are all mine and someday I will do a wonderful project with lots of buttons and buttonholes all over it. I have even kept each one with the name of the person who gave it to me. Who knows? Maybe I'll be able to work that into the piece." —Debbie Casteel, owner of Aardvark Adventures (Livermore, Calif.)

Index

181

Appendices

Footnotes

Chapter 3

[1] Anderson, Joseph, ed. *The Town and City of Waterbury, Connecticut*, vol. 2. New Haven: Price and Lee Co., 1896, p. 275.

[2] Luscomb, Sally, and Cassidy, Ethel. *The Old Button Box.* Southington, Conn.: Quiz Industries, 1951.

Chapter 4

[3] Jensen, Doreen, and Sargent, Polly. *Robes of Power: Totem Poles on Cloth.* Vancouver: University of British Columbia Press, 1986, p. 78.

[4] Donnally, Trish. "Designer Brings Fun to High Fashion." *San Francisco Chronicle*, July 29, 1988, p. 1.

[5] Johnson, Bonnie. "In Paris, His Slinky Dresses Have Made Mississippi-Born Designer Patrick Kelly the New King of Cling." *People Weekly*, June 15, 1987, p. 112.

Chapter 6

[7] Holme, Charles, ed. *Peasant Art in Sweden, Lapland and Iceland.* London: The Studio, Ltd., 1910.

Odd Facts

[6] McNulty, Faith. "Children's Books for Christmas." *The New Yorker*, November 30, 1987, p. 137.

[8] Glynn, Prudence. *In Fashion: Dress in the Twentieth Century.* New York: Oxford University Press, 1978, p. 130.

OUR PRECIOUS
DARLING
BUTTON
IN HIS CARE

Pet's Rest
Pet Cemetery
Colma, CA   1990

Are you interested in a quarterly newsletter about creative uses of the sewing machine, serger, and knitting machine? Write to The Creative Machine-bu, PO Box 2634, Menlo Park, CA 94026.